So—What Now?

SO

What
Now
?

Timothy
Green
&
J. Wesley
Furlong

Celebrating My Identity in Christ

Beacon Hill Press of Kansas City
Kansas City, Missouri

Copyright 1999
by Beacon Hill Press of Kansas City

ISBN 083-411-8521

Printed in the
United States of America

Cover Design: Marie Tabler

Library of Congress Cataloging-in-Publication Data

Green, Timothy Mark, 1961-
    So, what now? : celebrating my identity in Christ / Timothy Green, J. Wesley Furlong.
    p. cm.
  ISBN 0-8341-1852-1 (pbk.)
  1. Christian life. 2. New church members—Religious life. I. Furlong, J. Wesley, 1977- II. Title.
  BV4501.2 .G7454 1999
  248.2—dc21

                                                                    99-31572
                                                                         CIP

10   9   8   7   6   5   4   3   2   1

Contents

Introduction

Where Do We Go From Here?

There was not a thing in the world that could have prepared him for this moment. Adam had read the magazines, studied the moves, and memorized the diagrams. For years he had dreamed of gliding through the air on his snowboard as photographers snapped their cameras below. He had imagined himself soaring out of the half-pipe and traversing down steep chutes. But all the preparation and dreaming could not do justice to what he was now seeing. The day he had been waiting for had finally arrived!

No one else in Adam's family quite shared his excitement. For his parents as well as his older sister, Alyssa, the comfort of the warm room was much more inviting than being the first in line at the ski lifts. For Adam, however, this day was the one for which he had been waiting, so he was out of the room before the sun came up. Although his first snowboarding lesson didn't begin for a couple of hours, he was ready to head up the mountain.

With one foot in the binding and the other pushing alongside, he stumbled onto the chair lift. The view was breathtaking; snowcapped mountains stretched as far as he could see. Trees that had only decorated his house at Christmas were lining the slopes. The higher the lift rose, the more exhilarated he became. At the top of the intimidating mountain peaks, snow swirled like a tornado. Far in the distance he could hear explosions as workers blasted away potential avalanches. As he stumbled off the chair lift, Adam's only question was how to stop once he started down. However, he figured that he could find out the answer to that question when the time came.

Without much hesitation, Adam leaned on his left foot and plunged down the slope. While people were traversing from side to side, he shot straight down the middle like a bullet. Suddenly he realized that the question of stopping might have been a little more important than he had originally thought. He was going too fast simply to fall over, and no end was in sight. As he made his way around a small bend, his worst nightmare stared him in the face. Without a care in the world and oblivious to the potential danger that was approaching, an older couple was poling across Adam's path. With Adam's having no clue how to turn or how to stop, the inevitable took place. As he collided into the man, poles and headgear went flying into the air. Although Adam's fall was neatly broken, neither the man nor his wife were too excited about Adam's sudden stop! Apologizing and giving the man back his gear, Adam proceeded down the mountain.

Having a few more minutes before his first lesson, Adam made his way to the snowboard park. All around him, snowboarders were flying 20 feet into the air. Others were doing 360-degree turns off picnic tables and slides. At the bottom of the park was Adam's ultimate challenge—the half-pipe! Taking a deep breath, he started to make his move to that ultimate challenge. Jumping safely onto a tabletop, he dropped back onto the packed snow. With a newfound confidence, he turned his eyes to the only other jump that separated him from the half-pipe. He watched as other snowboarders slowly traversed down the steep incline and then launched into the air, twisting and contorting their bodies. As he thought about whether or not he should go for the jump, he saw a man around his father's age successfully make an effortless jump. He said to himself, "If he can look that good, surely a 16-year-old will have no problem at all!"

Standing up and tightening his bindings, Adam shot straight down to the jump. In a split second his board was off the ground. As he wobbled through the air, he tried to straighten out his board. But it was too late. As he came crashing face first into the packed snow, Adam wondered for the first time, "Why in the world did I do this?" Wiping out in front of all those other snowboarders erased any desire he had to get back up. This one fall put all of his dreams into a new perspective. Every desire he had to "make it big" collapsed with that one fall. He began to think that staying comfortably indoors in front of the television with a bag of chips just *watching* the snowboarders was not that bad of an idea after all. It certainly would be safer!

Adam now had a choice to make. On one hand, he could go back down the mountain and return to *watching* snowboarders on television and *looking* at their moves in sports magazines. On the other hand, he could retrieve his board, find his instructor, and commit to the adventure for which he had been dreaming so long. Adam was faced with one of the most important questions he would confront as a snowboarder: "Where do I go from here? What happens now?"

Committed to his dream, Adam got off the ground, found his instructor, and began to learn the basics of snowboarding. The more he learned about snowboarding that morning, the more he thought, "If only I had known that this morning!" Following his first lesson, Adam met his family for lunch. After telling them how well his lessons had gone, his sister Alyssa popped the surprise question: "So, how did you do *before* your lesson?" Alyssa always seemed to know everything that was going on.

With a nervous smile he mentioned the collision, but seeing his parents' reaction, he replied, "I'll tell you the rest later."

Even though Adam got to be with his sister only a few times a year since she had entered college, she had become one of the most influential people in his life. Adam felt that he could trust her with anything. In fact, every once in a while Adam would give Alyssa a call at school when he was confused or uncertain about things. He particularly trusted her walk with the Lord. Even though Adam didn't consider himself a Christian, deep down he wanted to have what his sister had.

After a great week of conquering the mountain, Adam and his family headed back home. A few days later Alyssa returned to college for the spring semester. Adam started back to school, and life returned to normal. In the weeks that followed, Adam began to face some tough decisions. He particularly began to feel caught between two worlds. In one world he had to maintain the controls and keep the pieces of his life together. But as he looked at his sister's life, he saw another kind of world. Although she also had tough decisions and challenges, her life seemed so different.

Late one evening Adam gave Alyssa a call to find out what this difference was. She reminded Adam how a few years earlier she had entered into a trusting relationship with God. She told him that her moment-by-moment walk with God made all the difference in the world. Although

Adam could never quite understand just what Alyssa meant when she would say these things, he knew that she really did have a unique peace about life. He became increasingly curious about how a relationship with God would give that kind of peace.

As Alyssa's spring break approached, she began to tell Adam that she couldn't wait to give him a surprise present for his birthday. His mind raced with ideas of what it might be. He kept dropping hints about how much he would love to have his own snowboard. However, nothing could have prepared him for this surprise. When he opened the card, he didn't know quite how to respond. It definitely was not what he had been expecting, but Alyssa's smile was too bright for him not to act excited. She had purchased a week at summer church camp for him. She had already made the reservations, cleared his work schedule with his boss, and arranged the transportation. With no ready excuse coming to mind, Adam agreed to go.

That summer became the turning point in Adam's life. A few weeks after school ended, he headed off to his first church camp. The environment was different from anything he had experienced. At first he was a little skeptical and even felt a little out of place, but deep down there was an excitement about the week. Adam had a blast. With the exception of the shepherd's pie in the cafeteria and the cold showers in the mornings, everything was great. He especially enjoyed the tree swing that hovered over the cold water spring as well as the "blob," which propelled people up to 20 feet in the air. The afternoon of horseback riding was great as well. And definitely Adam would never forget those counselors, who just begged to be attacked with shaving cream and water balloons!

The biggest surprise of the week for Adam was the evening services. Although he had gone to church, he never really seemed to pay much attention. For some reason, this week his mind was more focused. As songs were sung, there was a passion that Adam had never heard before even on the radio. The speaker's words were amazing—about some other kind of world. In fact, the world the speaker talked about sounded a lot like the world Alyssa seemed to be living in. Several of the campers around Adam really appeared to know about and have a passion for this other world. Something about the music, the speaker, and many of the counselors and campers seemed to be real. Adam became captivated by what all was taking place each evening.

On the final evening, the speaker once more talked about this "other world." He spoke about the emptiness that every human being has and the way in which we all try to fill that emptiness with certain things, relationships, and personal accomplishments, yet how all of these attempts to provide life for ourselves ultimately fail. The speaker concluded by saying, "You've tried to fill that hole in your life with everything imaginable. You've tried to provide life for yourself for too long. Now's the time for you to give up the endless game and allow the One who gave you life in the first place, God, to fill that hole and to give you abundant life!"

Adam felt as if the speaker were talking directly to him. Adam knew what he needed to do, but the altar seemed to be a world away from the chair in which he was sitting, and there were a lot of unanswered questions in between.

With his head in his hands, Adam began to think about his life. Up to this point, his life really was in *his* own hands. He called the shots. He lived his life the way he wanted to. He provided the answers. If things were going to happen in his life, it was pretty much up to him to make them happen. He had often thought, "Why do I need somebody to 'save' me when there's nothing I need to be saved from? *I'm* in control of my life, and if trouble comes, *I* can take care of myself." But as Adam thought about his life that night, he could see the empty hole the speaker was talking about. If he were honest with himself, he would have to admit that he could not give life to himself no matter how hard he tried.

As the speaker gave the final invitation to come and pray, Adam decided that it was time for a radical change in his life. He stood to his feet and walked down to the front. Accepting God's love and forgiveness, he began what was to become an incredibly dynamic relationship with God. As Adam realized that he *really* was forgiven, all the guilt that he had ever felt over certain things he had said and done was erased. He felt that he had a whole new start to life. It was like being born all over again!

As Friday morning arrived, everyone said their goodbyes and hopped onto their vans and buses. Adam exchanged phone numbers and addresses with a few of his new friends. As the van drove down the bumpy road, leaving the campsite behind in a trail of dust, Adam promised himself and God that things were going to be different. That evening, before going to bed, Adam read several verses from the Bible and prayed. This week was definitely a turning point in Adam's life.

As the alarm clock went off early Saturday morning, Adam dreaded having to get out of bed. It was time to return to the *real world*. That real world arrived very quickly for Adam. Although he may have changed during that week of camp, nothing else seemed to have changed.

Work was still tough. Relationships still got complicated. Temptations still came. The future was still not certain. Many of the same struggles that Adam had dealt with before camp kept slapping him in the face. As time went on, long mornings at work and rigorous afternoon football practices exhausted Adam. Soon he was too tired to pray at night, and he slept in too late to pray in the mornings. Before he knew it, school was starting back, and it didn't take long for Adam to realize that he was no longer at church camp. When he told a couple of his friends what happened at summer camp, they just smiled and nodded their heads.

As the summer became more and more a distant memory, so did Adam's excitement about his newfound life. He even began to question if anything had really happened to him or if he just had another emotional high. He began to wonder if Christianity was nothing more than making a trip to an altar and reciting a sinner's prayer. His camp counselor had encouraged him to read the Bible and pray each day, but after a few weeks Bible reading and prayer became more of a chore that he *had* to do rather than something that he *wanted* to do. God didn't seem to talk back when he prayed, and the world of the Bible seemed to be galaxies away from his "real world."

Much like his first adventure on the snowboard when his face was pressed up against the packed snow, Adam now faced one of the most crucial decisions of his life. On one hand, he could give up. He could conclude that nothing really had happened at camp, it was all just an emotional high, or that he just wasn't able to be a Christian. He could make the choice to *watch* other people, like Alyssa, make the journey with God. On the other hand, he could commit to the great adventure of jour-

neying moment by moment with his Instructor and learn
from Him what this journey was all about. Adam was
faced with one of the most important questions that con-
fronts every Christian: "Where do I go from here? What
happens now?"

Being too committed to the dream of a lifelong journey with God to give up and knowing that something real
had taken place in his life, Adam got off the ground,
turned to his Instructor, and began to learn the basics of
what it really means to be a Christian. He began to see
how certain misunderstandings could become obstacles in
the journey. He also began to see just how important it
was to know and understand what really had happened
at camp and how to move forward from there.

Adam is certainly not the only person to have faced
the question "What happens now?" We all do. In the next
few pages, you are invited to a journey in which we will
attempt to answer the questions, "Where do we go from
here? What happens now?" These questions confront
every young Christian who desires to live out what began at a summer camp, in a revival service, at an altar,
or during a special time of prayer. After we *become* a
Christian, where do we go? Who are we? What are we
supposed to do?

As you read this book, allow our Instructor, the
Lord, to guide you and teach you. The pages you are
about to read are not our Instructor; however, they can
become one means our Instructor can use to help give
you a better understanding of the relationship that you
share with God.

The journey we make will begin by taking a look at
some of the common misunderstandings that we often
have about our walk with God. Since these misunderstandings can become detours and obstacles in our walk,

it's important for us to talk about them honestly. Our journey will continue by exploring what *really* happens when we enter into a relationship with God. We will discover that at the heart of what happens is a change in our very identity, a change in who we are! Our journey will conclude with a look at the way in which we celebrate our newfound identity in Jesus. The God who called you to start the journey in the first place promises to go with you as you make the journey. What lies ahead of us is the adventure of a lifetime!

Reflecting on Our Journey with God

1. Can you think of a time similar to Adam's snowboarding experience when you enjoyed the exhilaration of facing a challenge only to hit a dead end and ask, "What happens now?" What were your thoughts and feelings at that time?

2. How would you describe the time when you first came to realize God's love and forgiveness in your life? What were your thoughts and feelings at that time?

3. How would you describe your journey with God from the time you started until now?

4. In your journey with God, what victories are you celebrating now? What questions and challenges are you now facing?

Part 1
Facing the Obstacles

> *Not that I have already obtained this or have already reached the goal; but I press on to make it my own, because Christ Jesus has made me his own.*
>
> **—Philippians 3:12**

Looking for Another Quick Fix: The Obstacle of Fast-Food Religion

Following a long day of work, Adam decided to make a quick stop for something to eat before going to the basketball game. After ruling out the cafeteria and seeing that there wasn't enough time to sit down, he headed toward his old standby restaurant with the bright neon sign. As Adam pulled around to the side, a garbled voice came blaring over the speaker: "Do you have any coupons? May I take your order?"

Sticking his head out the window, Adam yelled back into the speaker, "Yeah—I'd like a triple cheeseburger with bacon, a double large order of fries, and . . ." Figuring that he might counteract all those fat grams, he concluded "and a diet cola!" The muffled voice came back over the speaker giving him the price.

As Adam pulled around to the pickup window, his appetite grew stronger by the moment. Opening up the window, the hostess gave Adam a friendly smile, repeated the price of the meal, and took his money. She came back quickly, gave him his change, and said, "Your order will be right up."

Adam hadn't realized how hungry he was until now. The only thing he had eaten all day was a couple of doughnuts on his way to work that morning.

Adam's fast-food nightmare was about to begin. The hostess had disappeared. After a couple of minutes, Adam tapped on the window, but nobody answered. As he saw the line inside moving quickly, he thought, "It would've been quicker to go inside." Even though he was usually pretty patient, he became restless. After several minutes, he looked on the window and saw a sign that read, "Got a complaint? Call 1-800. . . ." As he quickly jotted down the number, he thought, "This is ridiculous! This place is supposed to be *fast* food." His impatience grew with each second. After another minute or two, he banged the car horn, but nobody was listening. After placing the order, everything seemed to come to a screeching halt.

Finally, after about five minutes, there she was—the hostess with a brown bag in hand and a huge smile on her face. As if nothing wrong had happened, she opened the window and said, "Here's your order! Hope you enjoy your meal. Have a good day!"

As his car screeched out of the parking lot, Adam thought, "A good day? It *was* good until I had to wait half the day for a cheeseburger. What's the world coming to? I gave up five minutes of my day for *fast* food!"

Adam is by no means the first person to feel that way. Nothing is all that unique to Adam. In fact, we all live in a world of "fast food," and that world influences all our lives. Because fast remedies and rapid answers are important to us, we decide how well something works based upon how quickly it produces the results that we want. In our world of microwave dinners, fast-acting allergy medicines, E-mail, 10-minute oil changes, and ATMs, we eat rapidly, feel better quickly, reach a friend halfway around the world immediately, have our car serviced hastily, and get cash instantly! If we don't see rapid results, something must be broken. We buy products because they're "fast-acting," "quick," "immediate," and "instant."

This fast-food world is not limited to hamburgers, allergy relief, E-mail, oil changes, and instant cash. With quick fixes hitting us from every direction, we also see God as a fast-acting medication or as an ATM full of instant cash. Popular religion advertises that a "dose of God" will be a quick fix to the broken pieces of our life. We think that if we push all the right "God buttons," the "divine ATM" will give us rapid refunds. Often a trip to an altar, a summer camp, or a morning devotional can become much like a religious drive-thru. We place our order, tell God what we want, show Him the broken pieces, and ask Him to get rid of the weak things in our lives. Then we turn around and expect immediately to pick up God's "brown bag" of goodies that we can live on for the rest of our lives. Everything in our walk with God should be completed, we think. Getting up from an altar, leaving a campground, or finishing a devotional, we say to ourselves, "Now I'm finally there!"

Whose Problem Is This—Mine or God's?

One of the first obstacles Adam faced in his journey with God was this obstacle of "fast-food religion." The night that he prayed and accepted the forgiveness of God, Adam thought that the struggles and weaknesses that he had faced beforehand were all over. He thought that he had "arrived." When he woke up the first day back from camp and realized that he was still weak in certain areas of his life, that he still had the same temptations that he had experienced beforehand, and that he still was going to face obstacles and problems, he became frightened and bewildered. Early in his journey with God, Adam began to learn that God was not into a drive-thru fast-food religion of quick fixes and fast remedies. Adam realized that he had not "arrived."

Although we don't seem to talk much about "fast-food religion," this misconception is one many of us face early in our journey with God. When we don't see all the pieces of the puzzle fit perfectly together right away, we become discouraged with ourselves and impatient with God. We become frightened that either something is wrong with us or something is wrong with God. We even become paralyzed in the journey and unable to go any further. After a while, we may even become tempted just to give up.

So whose problem is it when we don't get the quick fix from God that we expected? Are we at fault? Could it be that we weren't serious enough when we prayed? Maybe we didn't say just the right words in our prayer? Perhaps we weren't focused enough. We decide that the next time we pray, we will be even *more serious.* We might even change our words or try harder at blocking out any outside thoughts that invade our mind. But in spite of all of our efforts at being serious, saying the right words, and having a single focus, the quick fix doesn't come. We still have weaknesses, we still face struggles, and we still have temptations.

Concluding that maybe we didn't commit enough to God when we prayed, we begin a never-ending guilt trip. We jump on the treadmill of "trying harder this time" and of making more and more promises to God if only He will deliver us and give us the quick fix. In all of these efforts, we believe that in some way *we* are responsible for making things happen rapidly and quickly. We think, "If I could just work *harder*, believe *greater*, pray *deeper*, and commit *more*, then God's quick fix will come!"

Make no mistake about it—believing, praying, and committing are essential practices in our journey with God. However, none of these were ever intended to be "magic potions" to control God. Instead, they are *responses* we make to God's love, forgiveness, and presence in our lives. When believing, praying, and committing become ways for us to get a "goody bag" of quick fixes from God, they are no longer our response to a God who loves us *first*. Instead, they become a way for us to pull God's strings as if He were our puppet. The journey with God ends up depending on *our* being "in charge!" We discover that the more we live by our own efforts and in our own strength, the more exhausted, discouraged, and guilt-ridden we become.

We try harder and harder to get our quick fix that will take care of every struggle, temptation, and weakness. However, one try simply leads to another. Our walk with God eventually becomes nothing more than a wild roller coaster of ups and downs. We feel that we're on fire for the Lord one day and cold as ice the next day. The more we experience these highs and lows, the more we see ourselves as spiritual failures. Sometimes we even come to the conclusion that while all of this "religion stuff" may be for other people, we're just not capable of having a consistent walk with God. So we give up.

Maybe the problem isn't with *us* at all. Could it be that the problem is with *God?* All kinds of questions about God begin to come to our mind. Is it possible that all of this "God stuff" is not everything that people make it out to be? Maybe all this talk about God's power to change lives is for just *some* people. Maybe some individuals are just better designed to walk with God than others are. Could it be that God plays favorites? We decide that while God hands over an assortment of quick fixes and rapid remedies to that girl in our youth group or to that older saint in our church, God just doesn't want to hand it over to us. Is it possible that some people just know how to "fake it" really well? Maybe God forgives our sins, but as far as real change goes, could it be that He isn't really all that interested in real-life transformation?

So when God's bag of quick fixes and rapid remedies doesn't show up, whose problem is it? Is it *our* problem? Is it *God's* problem? In a fast-food world, if the "goody bag" isn't stuffed full in a speedy matter of time, someone somewhere has got to be at fault. If we were doing what we should do and if God were working the way that He should work, then we would be much further along, living "happily ever after" with God's goody bag of quick fixes and rapid remedies held firmly in our hands.

What if the problem is *neither* with us *nor* with God? What if the problem is this fast-food mind-set that we have all bought into? It's amazing that we never even ask if *fast-food religion* is *really* God's way. We just assume that God is as much into fast food, quick fixes, and instant gratification as we are. As long as we think God lives in a fast-food world, we expect God to follow its rules. And as long as we expect God to follow fast-food rules, we will walk with God according to the rules of the up-and-down world of *fast-food religion*. We will keep looking for God to give us an easy-to-read map of our future, a handy list of "holy rules" for our everyday journey, a jolting emotional high for a lifetime, and a spiritual maturity like that of a person who has been walking with God for 50 years. At the same time, we will expect God to remove all temptations, to take away all the struggles that could defeat us, and to put all the scattered pieces of our life back together again overnight.

At Home in the World of Fast Food: Settling Down, Covering Up, and Giving Up

In the world of fast food, when temptations come, when God's direction for our lives is not immediately clear, when weakness and struggles hit us head-on, when memories from the past cast their shadows over us, or when the broken pieces of our lives are not rapidly glued back together, we grow impatient and become discouraged. Like Adam at the drive-thru window, we become frustrated with everybody around, including God and ourselves. Determined not to live the rest of our lives frustrated, we deal with our impatience, discouragement, and defeat and make up for not having "arrived" in different ways.

One of our first responses is simply to *settle down* where we are. Thinking that nothing else is really going to change in our lives, we just *accept* the way things are. We conclude that God must have given us everything He planned to give us. We find a comfort zone and decide just to maintain things the way they are. However, deep in our hearts we are hungry for God to continue to change the way we think and the way we live.

Other times when we don't see quick fixes and rapid results, we play the addictive game of *cover-up.* Thinking that we have "waited at the window" long enough, we settle for the way things are in our life, but at the same time we find ways to put on masks and disguises. We learn to be comfortable with *pretending* that everything in our walk with God is all together. In order to keep the game of cover-up going, we become dependent upon our own strength. Our walk with God rapidly becomes a cycle of playing the part of something that we are not. Like a treadmill that won't stop, our walk with God becomes a matter of trying harder and harder in our strength to live up to the way we want to be. However, the harder we try and the more we cover up, the more exhausted we become.

Discouraged by settling for the way things are and worn out by covering up, we conclude that any further change is just not possible. We tried, and then we tried harder. We pretended, and then we pretended harder. We committed, and then we committed harder. Ultimately we're tempted to throw our hands in the air and say, "I just can't do it anymore—I give up!"

The cycle of *settling down, covering up, and giving up* is repeated over and over by many of us who think that God is into fast-food religion. As long as we come to God the way we come to an ATM, making quick deposits and rapid withdrawals, we set ourselves up for discouragement and failure. As long as the altar, a summer camp, or a morning devotional is nothing more than a quick fix, we'll never know what God really desires for us. So does God really follow the rules of fast-food religion? Is God into quick fixes and rapid refunds as much as we are?

Pitch a Tent, Read a Map—or Get on the Road!

In order to get an answer to the previous question, one of the best places to turn is to the stories of our ancestors. In these accounts we see a world very different from ours. Take for example the story of Abraham and Sarah. At the outset, God makes them an incredible promise. He promises that their lives would not be based upon their performance or their achievements. Instead, their lives would simply be a *gift.* In particular God promises them land and children. In response to this promise, Abraham and Sarah are simply to trust that God will keep His promise.

God instructs Abraham and Sarah to leave their homeland and to set out on a journey. However, He never tells them to arrive *quickly* at a distant destination, to pitch a tent there, and to settle down. His concern is *not* that Abraham and Sarah immediately arrive at some designated spot. His concern is that they get on the road and *walk* with Him. He calls them to an ongoing journey that comes in the form of a trusting relationship. God would provide life for them, and they were to trust God for that life. Whenever Abraham and Sarah thought it was time to pitch a tent and settle down, God would tell them to move on!

Not only does God *not* tell Abraham and Sarah to arrive quickly at a distant destination—He also never hands them a road map. Instead, He promises them His presence. It is as if He says to them, "Just get on the road and go! One thing you can count on: I will be with you all along the way." Why would they need a road map if they have the Mapmaker with them every step they take? Step by step, moment by moment, hand in hand with God, Abraham and Sarah travel into the future.

However, when God's promise exploded into Abraham and Sarah's lives, they tried to help God out in order to get quickly to their final destination. Just like them, we also want to get "there" immediately, wherever that might be.

What makes our walk with God different from fast-food religion is our dependence. We don't depend upon the altar at which we prayed; our trust is not in the summer camp at which we first came to know God; and our faith is not in our morning devotion time. Ultimately our trust, our faith, and our dependence is never in what we can do and accomplish, nor is it in where we can finally arrive. Our trust, our faith, and our dependence are always in *the God who loves us, forgives us, and calls us to go with Him on a lifelong journey!*

God calls us to get off the cycle of "trying harder." We've made the initial step on a journey, but now that journey continues. It's a journey of *trust* in God and God alone. God says to us, "Go!" And He goes with us. As we journey forward with God, *God* changes us, heals us, instructs us, and guides us. Step by step, stage by stage, moment by moment, God continues what *He himself* started in our lives.

While fast-food religion sees "getting there" as picking up an assortment of maps, rules, and jolts, God sees "getting there" as the journey we daily share with Him and with others on the same road. While fast-food religion is comfortable with a static religion of getting a ticket stamped that will get us into heaven and then going through the motions, God calls us to join Him in a dynamic, continuing, and growing relationship. Beginning with where we are, God goes with us all along the way! He daily gives us fresh bread and flowing water.

So what happened at that altar, in that camp, during that prayer time, or in that morning devotional time? Did nothing really change? Oh, you'd better believe something changed—the most incredible change in the world took place! It involved your very identity. You became a whole new person on a whole new journey with a whole new citizenship in a whole new community! But you didn't *arrive* at your final destination; you *started* the journey. Paul describes it this way: "Not that I have already obtained this or have already reached the goal; but I press on to make it my own, because Christ Jesus has made me his own. Beloved, I do not consider that I have made it my own; but this one thing I do: forgetting what lies behind and straining forward to what lies ahead, I press on toward the goal for the prize of the heavenly call of God in Christ Jesus" (Philippians 3:12-14).

Reflecting on Our Journey with God

1. What are some of the quick fixes, easy answers, and rapid answers that we turn to in everyday life?

2. In what ways do we tend to use God as a quick fix in our lives?

3. When God doesn't seem to provide a quick fix or rapid answer as soon as we want, how do we usually respond?

4. As you continue to journey with God, how might He be calling you to give up the search for quick fixes and go on by celebrating a lifelong growing, dynamic relationship with Him?

5. To further explore what the Bible says about the journey we share with God, read Genesis 12:1-9; Joshua 1:1-9; Philippians 3:12-16; Hebrews 5:11—6:2; 11:13-16; and 12:1-2.

I am reminded of your sincere faith,
a faith that lived first in your
grandmother Lois and your mother
Eunice and now, I am sure, lives in you.
—2 Timothy 1:5

All Dressed Up but Nowhere to Go: The Obstacle of Family Tree Religion

As Adam was mowing the lawn late one afternoon, he looked up and saw his three-year-old neighbor, Sophie. She was trying everything possible to get his attention. Apparently she had spent the last several hours rummaging through her mother's makeup cabinet and closet. With powder all over her, polish streaked across her hands, and perfume stronger than the smell of the freshly cut grass, Sophie showed off a dress that dragged about three feet behind her. Decked out with half a dozen strands of big, bright, gaudy beads and wearing shoes with three-inch heels, she clumsily came running to Adam. As Adam turned the mower off, he heard her yelling, "I'm a mommy now! I'm a mommy now! Adam, I'm a mommy now."

Trying to hold back his laughter, Adam replied, "Why are you a mommy?"

Puzzled by his question, Sophie answered with confidence, "Look at me, Adam. I have big people's clothes, big people's shoes, and big people's makeup. I'm a mommy!"

Nodding in agreement, Adam thought, "Poor Sophie—she's all dressed up with nowhere to go."

While the game of "dress up" seems to be a part of most kids' early years, it isn't just a kids' game. In fact, we all seem to play it throughout our lives. Many times the only way we know how to act in different situations is based upon what we've seen other people do in those same situations. If we're an athlete, then we *act* like athletes we admire; if we're a teacher, then we *act* like our teachers; and if we're a parent, then we *act* like our parents.

Soon after Adam returned home from camp, he faced the obstacle of the religious game of "dress up." Everything he knew about God had come from a few important people in his life, people like Alyssa, his parents, a pastor, a couple of youth pastors, a Sunday School teacher, and two or three of his friends. Since these people had pointed the way to Christ, he just assumed that he had finally "bought into" their religion at camp. He was accepting their beliefs, mimicking their actions, and speaking their language. Because these important individuals modeled the Christian life for him, this response was natural and even good.

However, Adam, like all of us, soon came to a point in his walk with God in which he began to ask, "What am I supposed to do with the faith of these important models, teachers, and friends in my life?" Simply mimicking these people made him feel that he was always one step removed from God. He began to feel that these people actually had a relationship with God, while he was just going through the motions of the way *they* lived. Like Sophie, he felt all "dressed up"—he looked the part, played the part, and talked the part—but he seemed to be going nowhere. He began to realize that playing the part of a Christian didn't *make* him a Christian any more than "dressing up" made Sophie a mother. Instead, his beliefs, his actions, and his language came first from *being* a Christian. What he did came from *who he was!*

Like Adam, when our walk with God becomes no more than our own attempt to mimic a Christian role model, the journey becomes static. We begin to feel as if we're simply going through the motions. Sometimes we even feel that we're playing a game rather than being real. We feel very religious, but a dynamic, growing relationship with God seems to be light-years away. So if God really does desire for us to be in a dynamic relationship with Him, what do we do with "family tree religion"? What place do role models and mentors have in our lives?

Priestly Youth Pastors and Godly Family Members

Most people would not call him a youth pastor, but to Samuel a youth pastor was pretty much what Eli was. Eli was definitely one of God's greatest gifts to Samuel. He was a model, a friend, a mentor, and a teacher. He was there to listen to Samuel's questions, and he was there to provide answers.

When God began to call Samuel, Samuel's response was very natural. He would quickly run to Eli and say, "Here I am—you called me." (See 1 Samuel 3:1-11.)

Each time, Eli would answer, "I didn't call you; go back to bed." After Samuel came to him several more times like this, Eli realized that God must be calling

Samuel, so he finally said to him, "The next time He calls you, you simply say, 'Speak, Lord—your servant is listening'" (1 Samuel 3:9, author's paraphrase).

The next time God called, Samuel didn't run to Eli; instead, he responded to God. Without Eli, Samuel would not have known what to do. Eli played the very important role of pointing Samuel to God.

But it was not enough for Samuel simply to keep running to his role model. Ultimately Samuel responded to God himself. Only then could he really discover God's calling in his life.

Timothy had an incredible Christian heritage. Both his mother, Eunice, and his grandmother Lois were followers of Jesus. However, God was now calling Timothy to something deeper and more dynamic than to mimic his family members. While God had done wonderful things in the lives of Timothy's family, He was now wanting to do something in Timothy's life. In a letter to Timothy, Timothy's mentor, Paul, exclaimed, "I know about the faith of your mother and of your grandmother, but I am certain that faith is now also in *you*. Therefore, fan into flame the gift of God that is in you" (2 Timothy 1:5-6, author's paraphrase). Paul was encouraging Timothy to allow the spark of faith that had been ignited in Timothy's life by faithful family members to burst into a huge flame. Timothy was to make the faith of his family his own.

The Role of Our Mentors: Pointers Rather than Crutches

So what do the stories of Samuel and Timothy say about role models and mentors? God has always used significant people like family members, pastors, teachers, and peers to point the way to Him. These people never simply point to themselves; they are always pointers to Someone and something *beyond themselves.* When our journey consists of simply mimicking our mentors and role models, these incredible gifts from God can become crutches for us rather than pointers. Sometimes it becomes easy for us to lean blindly on them. We copy their ways, buy into their beliefs, and use their language without ever discovering why they act the way they act, believe what they believe, and say what they say. Why is it so easy for us to use our role models as crutches? Why might we hold on to the religion of our mentors without ever allowing their faith to become our own?

Sometimes we stop short because of our own spiritual insecurities. Clinging to the religion of others can be like holding on to a security blanket. As we watch the faith of strong people, we feel comfortable, safe, and protected. So we settle for observing *their* strong belief in God. However, in our journey with God, we're challenged to move beyond the familiar and comfortable world that we can control and feel safe in. Although watching the religion of role models and mentors from the sidelines *seems* easier than getting into the adventure ourselves, we end up missing the journey that we could be making alongside them.

Other times we stop short because of our age. We think we're just "too young." Seeing the "serious" Christian life as something for older adults, we might think, "Hey—I'm only a teen! Someday, when I have everything figured out, I'll go on a 'mature walk' with God. Until then, I'll stay in the crib." However, there never will be a time when we have *everything* figured out. As soon as one set of questions is answered, there will always be another set of questions that come up. What God has for us has nothing to do with when we're "old enough" or "mature enough." It has everything to do with what God wants to do in us and through us—*now!* Once again, Timothy's mentor, Paul, addressed the insecurity of age when he boldly said, "Don't let anybody look down on you because you are young, but *you* set an example in speech and conduct, in love, in faith, and in purity" (1 Timothy 4:12, author's paraphrase).

Other times we may stop short because we see our own weaknesses or inadequacies. We say to ourselves, "I'm not quite strong enough yet! When I get all these struggles straightened out, or when I overcome that nagging temptation, or when I . . ." and the list goes on and on. However, God does not call us into this journey based upon how strong or adequate we are. If we wait until we're "strong enough" to make the faith our own, we'll always be waiting for tomorrow. If we wait until our struggles and temptations are overcome, we will wait a lifetime. God calls us actively to set out on this journey and make the faith our own *right where we are now.*

At other times our "holding on" to the religion of other people and "holding back" on getting into the journey is related to a misunderstanding about God. For some of us, God represents a distant and lifeless religious system full of duties and behaviors. Following God is nothing more than carrying out those responsibilities without ever thinking about them. If we have a mentor to follow, we can think even less about those responsibilities. We just put ourselves into "automatic pilot" and do what our mentor does, say what our mentor says, and go where our mentor goes. However, God does not call us into a static, dead, remote world of religious duties. Rather, He invites us to join Him in an incredibly dynamic relationship.

So if our role models and mentors are not "crutches" in the journey, what are they? Definitely some of God's most incredible gifts to us are the significant people who point us to God. They instruct us; they motivate and encourage us; they challenge and correct us. However, whether they be persons in the Bible, persons who have lived before us, or persons who are alive today, our mentors and role models are not there to squeeze us into their mold so that we come out looking, acting, and talking just like them. They provide us with a *pattern* to follow.

Imagine that you were shown the following arrangement of numbers: "2-4-6-8 . . ." Next you were shown the number 4,006 and, based upon the first arrangement of numbers, you were asked what number would follow 4,006. You would likely answer 4,008. Why? Because you saw a pattern, and based upon that pattern, you knew what to do thousands of numbers later. In the same way, our mentors and role models provide us with a pattern. We do not simply repeat "2-4-6-8" all over again. At 4,006 we know what to do next because the pattern has been established. We do not go back and duplicate our mentors' and role models' lives like clones, but we live out the pattern they have set before us. Based on that pattern, we move on in our journey with God. With this incredible "cloud of witnesses," we push on to run the race ourselves!

The pattern given to us by role models and mentors becomes extremely important in going on in our journey with God. What they believe, the way they act, and the language they use shapes what we believe, the way we act, and the language we use. But in order for us to do more than go through the motions, it is important for us to sit down with our family members, mentors, teachers, and pastors and to ask them about the pattern that we see in their lives. *Why* do we act the way we act? *Why* do we say the things we say? *Why* do we believe what we believe? What do we mean by certain words? God is not into a rote religion in which we get everything down pat and never think about our beliefs, our actions, or our language. God desires that what we believe, do, and say come from our hearts and our minds. Ultimately what we believe, what we do, and what we say come from *who we are*. Our role models and mentors teach us and remind us over and over again of who we are! Knowing who we are, we move forward *together*.

Going On

God challenges you to "go on." He calls you to move from the comfort and security of your spiritual nest and to soar into the adventure of a lifelong journey with Him and with fellow travelers, including your mentors. Throughout the journey, God will provide significant people who will remind you of your identity and who will provide the pattern to follow. But make no mistake about it—these people provide a pattern for the journey; they are *not* a substitute for the journey. You are called to make the faith of family members, teachers, pastors, and peers your faith. You are called to do more than observe somebody else's religion; you are invited to join them. You share a relationship with God and with other people on the journey so that you are a participant in the very same faith in which your role models and mentors participate. With one hand clasped in the hands of our mentors and role models, our other hand reaches out to the God to whom they have pointed us. God desires that the spark of faith in you be ignited into a huge flame. He desires not that you be "dressed up" with nowhere to go; He desires for you to "get on the road" with Him and go.

⚠ Reflecting on Our Journey with God

1. As you have grown up, in what ways have you pat-
   terned your life after other people?

2. Who are those significant role models and mentors in
   your walk with God? What have you seen in their
   lives that points you to a walk with God?

3. Why might we feel safer simply to go through the motions of mimicking the religion of certain people rather
   than sharing in a dynamic relationship with God?

4. In the journey that you are making with God, how
   might God be challenging you to go on now and to fan
   into flame the spark that is in you, making the faith
   of significant mentors in your life your own faith?

5. To further explore what the Bible says about the relationship we share with God, read 1 Samuel 3:1-11; 2 Timothy 1:3-7; Philippians 3:4-11; Romans 8:14-17; and Galatians 4:6-9.

Do not be conformed to this world, but be transformed by the renewing of your minds, so that you may discern what is the will of God—what is good and acceptable and perfect.

—Romans 12:2

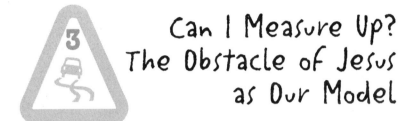

Can I Measure Up? The Obstacle of Jesus as Our Model

Realizing that he was into something much bigger than mimicking the religion of significant mentors in his life, Adam decided that if he were to imitate anyone, that person should be Jesus. Jesus would become his "supreme Hero."

Adam already knew what it meant to have a hero in his life. For several years now, his hero had been one of the best Norwegian snowboarders who had ever braved a mountain. This man, Terje Haakonsen, did things on the snowboard that would leave spectators spellbound and competitors breathless. Adam could always count on his hero to push the limits and to attempt the impossible. But Terje was even more than a hero to Adam. Ultimately, he represented Adam's dream of accomplishing what he himself wanted terribly. Having studied his model's unique style and followed his every move, Adam knew that if he were ever to be a good snowboarder, he would have to imitate Terje.

Heroes and role models are not unique to Adam, of course. Most all of us have those persons we aspire to be like. Early in our lives we're introduced to various persons who represent success in their fields. Moreover, throughout our lives we're bombarded by those larger-than-life characters who possess what we're after and who live out our dream of success. Whether in sports, music, business, drama, or everyday life, these people represent an ideal for us. They serve as motivation behind hours of practice, study, and preparation. Like the picture on the front of a jigsaw puzzle box, they represent what we ultimately want when we've put all of the pieces of our life together.

As Adam became serious about his walk with God, it was no surprise that he decided to make Jesus his ultimate superhero and role model. Determined that from now on Jesus would be *the* One he would strive to be like, Adam resolved that he would say what Jesus would say, go where Jesus would go, and do what Jesus would do. He determined that he would do everything within his power to be like Jesus.

As fitting as it was for Adam to make Jesus his model, his misunderstanding of what it meant to be like Jesus became an obstacle for a growing walk with God. This misunderstanding becomes an obstacle for many of us in our journey.

Who Is Really in Control in a World of Achievement?

Make no mistake about it—our goal on the journey with God is definitely to be like Jesus. But for Adam it became a personal task of trying harder and achieving more. Anytime our walk with God is based upon our *own* ability to perform and measure up, we run head-on into an obstacle that can become a potential pitfall. In all our attempts at performance, *we* are the ones in charge. Christlikeness ends up becoming something we try to bring about ourselves. We fail to realize that God is the one who is changing us into the likeness of Jesus.

As we grew up, our acceptance by others was often based upon our achievements and performance. We all knew that the kid who was picked last for the team would never receive the same applause as the one who was chosen first. Why was that? Because the "first pick" seemed to have the greater ability to perform, and applause was always based upon performance. From sports to music, from schoolwork to church, we learned early on that if we pushed the right buttons, met the right expectations, pulled the right strings, and beat out the right people, we would be accepted and would receive the applause. We knew that if we did our homework and studied hard, we would get a good grade. If we went through a daily workout and regularly showed up for practice, we would get the starting position. If we rehearsed daily and took on tough compositions, we would get first chair. We also knew that if we failed to achieve, we might be left out, turned down, ridiculed, or even punished. Learning early on that success is based on how well we achieve, we were determined to put the pieces together just right. What better way to put the pieces together than to pattern after people who have been successful? And what better way to be successful in our walk with God than to pattern our lives after Jesus?

With Jesus as our model, this achievement-oriented mind-set can have a huge influence on our walk with God. Since we base our success on how well we perform like our heroes in music, sports, and drama, we link our success as a Christian to our ability to perform the way

Jesus would. If we can achieve a certain standard we've set for ourselves, then we believe that we will be acceptable. On the other hand, if we fail to meet that standard, we think of moving off to the sidelines and perhaps even quitting. Feeling that we possess neither the strength nor the willpower to live like Jesus, we find it much easier to give up. Not wanting to be branded with the scarlet letter "hypocrite" and not willing to risk failure, we decide not even to try anymore.

The obstacle with this achievement-oriented approach to Christlikeness is where it begins and where it ends. Because we begin with *our* being in ultimate control of *our Christlikeness,* we end up building a world in which *we* are still at the center. The driving force that lies behind our walk with God can be summed up in the popular phrase "If it's going to be, then it's up to me!" When *we* are the starting point for the Christian life, we end up building a world based upon what *we* can accomplish in our *own* willpower. God may be our "copilot" helping us along the way, but the controls continue to be in our hands. Becoming exhausted in *trying* to be like Jesus, we often either give up trying to live the Christian life because it is too difficult or we settle for carrying a burden that we were never intended to carry.

This point of exhaustion is exactly where Adam found himself in his walk with God. The harder he tried in his own power to be like Jesus, the more empty and self-defeating his walk became. He decided to give Alyssa a call. After hearing his explanation, she told him about her best friend in high school. Her real name was Regina Baldwin, but everyone at school just called her Gina. Although Gina had never ventured outside the invisible wall surrounding her city, she had shared her dream with Alyssa. Gina would tell Alyssa that someday she was going to "break out of that wall" and have her own house with a picket fence way out in the country. With a broad smile on her face, Gina would say, "I'm even going to have a dog that will meet the mailman and chase his truck all the way down the winding, dirt road." The fence in Gina's dream was more for appearance than protection; the dog in her dream was more for companionship than security. She dreamed of providing a place for her children where they could play outside without her worrying about drive-by shootings. However, the poverty, crime, and constant sound of sirens would always bring Gina out of her dream and back to reality.

Repeatedly Gina would say to herself, "If there's any hope of making it outside this invisible wall, it will be up to me!" She was ready to take full responsibility for making her dream come true. Knowing that nothing in this world was free and that her dream was never going to just fall from the sky, she knew that she was going to have to make her dream happen. With everybody counting on her to make the dream come true, she had incredible pressure to perform, and she didn't want to let anybody down. Teachers were looking at her test scores. Universities were looking at her transcript. Employers were looking at her résumé. Friends were looking at her personality. Her mom was looking at her paycheck. Even the church seemed to be looking at her attendance record and involvement. It seemed that no one looked at her for *who she was,* only for what she could offer and achieve. Everything seemed to have the "string of performance" attached to it.

This "string of performance" even seemed to be attached to God's acceptance of her. Ever since Gina had given her life to the Lord at a youth rally she had attended with Alyssa, Gina had tried as hard as possible to be as much like Jesus as she could be. She put reminders in her room; she even wore several reminders so she would remember to "perform" adequately for God. She finally became so exhausted by trying harder and pushing for God's acceptance that she was ready to give up.

As Alyssa told Gina's story to Adam, he could see himself exactly. Like Gina, he also was beginning to measure God's acceptance by how well he performed and by what he accomplished. The more he saw his journey with God as based upon what he could achieve, the more he viewed God as a distant and remote judge who rated him on his performance. Reading the Bible had become nothing more than looking into a mirror to see his short-comings. Increasingly, his life became more of a guilt trip for *not* achieving than it was a dynamic journey with God. His walk with God had become the maddening exercise of making it to a finish line that he could never quite reach. His trust was more in what he could do himself than in what God could do in him. More and more, he was living his life as if trying hard enough, witnessing to the right number of people, having devotions, performing the right acts, and attending church several times a week made him acceptable to God. It was as if he were now attempting to earn the gift of God's love that he had already received. As Jesus became nothing more than a superhero to imitate in his own strength, Adam's walk with God simply revolved around what he could achieve and how well he could perform. He finally became exhausted trying to *be like Jesus* in his own willpower and strength.

Measuring Up to a Model on the Outside

Gina and Adam are certainly not the first people to perform for God in their own strength. Many centuries ago, our ancestors would put reminders throughout their houses and on their bodies in order to remind them how to act. Can you imagine going to school with reminders pasted to your body? However, all the reminders in the world were not powerful enough to bring about *real* change in how they thought. Like us, our ancestors also had regular reforms and revivals to "get charged up," but the battery would soon die each time. Regardless of how many Scripture verses were hanging on their walls or from their clothes or above their doors, they kept failing in their actions. No matter how hard they tried, they couldn't change their ways any more than a spotted leopard can remove its spots. If their actions were ever to be what God desired, something more than outward reminders and regular revivals had to take place. The way they acted was *not* first the result of measuring up to an outward standard. Their actions were first the result of the way they thought. Therefore, what was needed for our ancestors was not another list of things to do and not to do; what was needed was a whole new way of thinking, a whole new mind-set. Ultimately, their *minds* had to be changed!

Our ancestors are not alone. Like both Adam and Gina, we all attempt to find ways to remind us how to act, and then we try everything within our power to "be like Jesus." Even today we often place reminders in our rooms and attach reminders to our bodies. We establish ways of behaving that are "Christlike," and then we try our hardest to carry out those ways.

However, this way of trying to be like Jesus by "gluing" Christlike behavior on to our lives works backward! If someone were to ask you if a plastic piece of fruit would grow if it were glued to a tree, you would answer, "That's ridiculous! Of course not. You can't just glue a piece of fruit on a tree and expect it to grow. The fruit must come naturally from the tree." However, we try to do the same thing in our walk with God. Once we come to Christ, we attempt to "glue" fruit on to the tree of our lives. We attempt to "be Christian" *without* Christ's doing anything. We act as if the Christian life is all up to us.

The Bible talks about the *fruit* of God's Spirit in our lives: "love, joy, peace, patience, kindness, generosity, faithfulness, gentleness, and self-control" (Galatians 5:22-23). We describe these characteristics as "Christ-likeness." However, we often attempt to "glue" this fruit on to our lives by trying harder to love, to be joyful, to be patient, to be kind, to be self-controlled, and so on. But in the same way that fruit is a *product* or a *result* that comes from *what a tree is,* the fruit of the Spirit is the *product* or *result* of *who we are* as a result of our relationship with God. As Christ is working in our lives, the *fruit* is naturally produced.

The Alternative to Performance— Walking with God

So if we don't simply set Jesus up as a superhero whom we try harder to be like, how *do* we become like Christ? How is the fruit produced if we don't "glue it on" to our lives? As Alyssa continued to tell Adam the story of Gina, Adam came to understand the alternative to a life of performance. In this alternative, real and authentic fruit *grows!*

Having tried as hard as she could to perform for God, Gina was finally exhausted. Ready to give up her walk with the Lord, she asked Alyssa to meet her after school for a few minutes. When they met, they read a devotional that was based on two scriptures, Genesis 17:1 and 1 John 1:7. The first scripture was God talking to Abraham. God said something like *"Walk* in My presence, and you'll be complete" (author's paraphrase). The other scripture said, "If we *walk* in the light as he himself is in the light, we have fellowship with one another, and the blood of Jesus his Son cleanses us from all sin" (italics added). Completeness, fellowship, and forgiveness were exactly what Gina had been looking for. In fact, she had become exhausted striving for these things. But what produced them was amazing. The answer was *not* in trying to do something in her own strength. The answer was found by a continual *walk with God!*

Gina couldn't get past the word "walk." To walk *with* someone was an activity involving a relationship. To Gina, walking meant spending time with another person. To walk with someone was to be in the presence of that person. These passages seemed to be talking about an ongoing, trusting relationship that God wants to have with His children. It had been easy for Gina to see God in the same way that she saw other people for whom she performed. God was simply a remote judge who rated her on how well she did. But a God who wanted to share a trusting *walk* with her was a whole new idea! Suddenly everything she had ever thought about God was rearranged. Gina began to understand that *being* Christian is *first* about a walk, an ongoing relationship, with God. It was not first about how well she could perform in her strength or what she could accomplish in her own willpower. She began to understand that only as she lived in the presence of Christ would she ever come to be like Jesus. Christlikeness does not come from our own attempts at *trying* to be like a model on the outside; it comes from living moment by moment in a trusting relationship with Him. As we continue to walk with Him, He continues to transform the way we think. In fact, our minds are being changed to the very mind of Jesus Christ. "Christlike actions" then result from this new way of "Christlike thinking."

As Adam heard about Gina's awakening, he began to see things much more clearly. He came to understand what the Bible means when it speaks of being able to know the good and perfect will of God as our *minds* are being renewed. No matter how hard he would try to clean up his own life, his attempts would never be enough. God was calling him to something deeper than *trying* harder in his strength to be like Jesus. God was calling him to a mind change, and as Adam *walked* in the presence of Christ, his mind would be changed!

What makes us Christlike is not what we can accomplish and perform in our own power. In simply trying harder or coming up with more effective strategies to be like Jesus, *we* still maintain the controls ourselves. We do not make ourselves Christlike; God makes us Christlike. As we live in a trusting relationship with God, *He* transforms us into the likeness of Jesus. The deeds we do, the words we say, and the places we go will be the result of that trusting relationship. God's first interest is not in *our ability* to perform but in *our availability* to be transformed! God does not work from the outside in; He works from the *inside* out.

So then is Jesus not our model? Oh yes, indeed He is! As we have said, we are being transformed into the very likeness of Jesus. Our calling is definitely to be like Jesus! But Jesus is a very different kind of model from our superheroes. He is not a model that remains outside of us and that we "try harder" to be like. We are not called simply to carry out the deeds of Jesus; we are called to have the mind of Jesus. We are called to see the world the way Jesus saw the world. We are called to have the perspective of Jesus. As we live in God's presence, God changes our minds, our vision, and our perspective. And as our minds are transformed, the fruit that we produce will not be plastic, but real!

Reflecting on Our Journey with God

1. Who are some of the heroes or models in everyday life after whom people tend to pattern their lives?

2. What particular qualities about the life of Jesus do we often try to imitate?

3. Why do we face a struggle when we try to do what Jesus would do without first sharing in the mind of Jesus? When we do this, why would we feel either as if the harder we try the more we face a dead end, or as if we have a foot in two worlds—God's world and our own?

4. In your journey with God, how might He be inviting you to go on and allow Him to continue to transform your mind into the mind of Jesus Christ?

5. To further explore what the Bible says about the change in our minds that God desires to make, read Deuteronomy 30:6-14; Jeremiah 31:31-34; Romans 8:1-11; 12:1-2; Philippians 2:1-11; 1 Corinthians 2:10-16; and 1 Peter 1:13-16.

Abide in me as I abide in you. Just as the branch cannot bear fruit by itself unless it abides in the vine, neither can you unless you abide in me.

—John 15:4

The Collision of Two Worlds: The Obstacle of Making Jesus "Fit" into Our World

For a junior who had played only one year of high school football, Adam had a good chance at the starting position, and he wanted desperately to be the starting defensive end for the opening game. The thought of leading the stampede through the paper sign as the cheerleaders shouted his name kept him motivated during those long summer workouts.

About two weeks before the "jamboree," the team was going through a routine practice when a not-so-routine event took place. As Adam ran across the middle of the field, the quarterback threw a pass over his head. Instinctively, Adam jumped for the ball. As soon as Adam leaped off the ground, the outside linebacker took Adam's legs out from under him, flipping Adam onto his head. Afterward, everything became blurry. Looking up, he saw people huddled around him. Although their mouths were moving, he could hear nothing.

Once Adam regained consciousness, his teammates carefully lifted him off the field. After running him through several tests, the team's trainer gave him the option either to return to the locker room and "doctor himself" or to go to the hospital to be checked out by a doctor.

With some encouragement from his coach, Adam decided to go to the hospital. Fortunately, he walked away with only a broken collarbone. Adam knew that he could have stayed in the comfort zone of the locker room to take care of himself. However, he realized that he had made a wise decision when he stepped into the unfamiliar world of the hospital, where someone knew much more about broken bones than he did. He had walked into the emergency room in pain and with questions, but he walked away with a diagnosis, a treatment, and an appointment for a checkup.

However, as Adam looked back over his journey with God, he realized that he wasn't being so wise. In fact, in many ways Adam was "taking care of himself." God was becoming more and more like a "spiritual medication" that Adam could use to fix his relationships, to answer his questions, to secure his future, and to remedy his sin. Adam had begun to find places to "plug God in" to his own familiar and comfortable world. In trying to make God fit into his *own* world, Adam faced an obstacle that many of us face in our journey. Two worlds began to collide. On one hand there was Adam's familiar and comfortable world; on the other hand there was God's world. Adam was now facing a common question for believers: would he attempt to "fix" his own life by continuing to "use" God like a medication, or would he place his life into the hands of the One who gave him that life to begin with? Ultimately, Adam was facing a matter of trust! Who was he finally going to trust with his life: himself or God?

Where Do We Turn with Life?

When things go wrong in our lives, we face the same choice that Adam had faced at the football game: attempt to "fix" things ourselves, or go to an expert. When our car breaks down, most of us have learned from experience that the last thing we want to do is fix it ourselves. When our computer crashes, the best option is most often to take it back to the company that produced it in the first place. Like a child who trusts a parent to fix a broken toy, we trust these "experts" to provide answers for what is broken.

Doctors take care of our bodies, and mechanics repair our cars, but what do we do with the brokenness of our lives? How do we find our way out when we hit a dead end and discover that we're lost? Where do we turn to find direction for relationships, for the future, and for handling temptation? Where do we go when we long for something that will last a lifetime and not just a moment? In dealing with the brokenness and sin of our lives, we have the same two options that Adam faced. On the one hand, we can try to handle everything ourselves. We can cover up, sweep the brokenness under the rug, rationalize our sin away, and do whatever else it takes to avoid seeing the brokenness in our lives. Our search for self-made remedies becomes much like wandering down a never-ending hallway in which we move from one empty room to another. Each room promises wholeness, security, freedom, acceptance, and life. However, no room is able to deliver on its promise. When we walk

out of each room, we're still in the same place we were
before we entered—trying to find somewhere to turn
with our lives. At the very center of this endless search
is our attempt somehow to maintain control over our
lives—to "take care of ourselves." On the other hand, we
can deal with the brokenness of our lives by turning to
the One who knows us best.

What Role Does God Play in *Your* World?

Believing that we are more than a cosmic mistake
and that God lovingly created us for a distinct purpose,
most of us finally come to realize somewhere in life that
we can no longer live our lives apart from God. After
having tried many of those empty rooms down that never-ending hallway, we turn to God with our lives. Once
we realize that God is a factor in our lives, we face the
crucial question, "So how will God *fit* into my life now?"

Often we seem to "sign God on" to our team roster
much like we would sign on a free agent. Once God is "on
our team," we can then use Him whenever we face diffi-
culties that we can't handle ourselves or when our first
plans fail. He serves as an amazing pinch hitter. Like a
heavenly Santa Claus, God is there as a reserve when all
our other resources have run dry. Like a "Dear Abby,"
God sits on our level and offers us kind advice and help
and even an occasional emotional boost. As a distant Creator who will someday judge the earth, God provides us
with eternal "fire insurance" to save us from hell and a
"free pass" to get us into heaven.

Wanting God to play a definite, active role in our
lives, we just don't want Him to play the lead role. That
role is reserved for us. In our hearts, we want God to be
a close enough part of our lives that we can use Him
when we need Him, but we want Him to be distant

enough that He doesn't quite take control of our lives. For sure—we believe in God; we just don't want our lives to be shaped by Him. Our journey can become something like sitting at a bargaining table with God. When He asks us to trust our lives to Him, we offer Him bits and pieces at a time.

In our relationship with God, we often desire an escape clause that will allow us to continue calling the shots and determining how we'll live our lives. While we deeply desire the benefits God can provide us, we want to hold on to the controls of the important decisions like jobs, friends, entertainment, and attitudes. These areas remain off-limits to God. As He calls us into a deeper walk with Him, we often tend to place certain conditions on our relationship: "I'll take the next step, *but* . . ." or "I'll continue farther *if* . . ." God is definitely a member of *our* team roster, but we still want to determine the lineup.

The Priority Puzzle

As we continue with God, we increasingly see the collision of two worlds: on one hand, our own familiar and comfortable world where we can keep "taking care of ourselves" and determine the lineup, and on the other hand, God's world. We finally begin to realize that God is going to have to be more than simply a reserve. He's more than one of many team members. We come to see God as an indispensable part of the team, ultimately the "top recruit." Realizing that we were never intended to play the part of God, we allow God to "take over." Offering Him the top position in our lives and first place on our priority list, we assume that we can then line up the other positions on the list. Overall, everything seems to work out well: God has what He deserves, and we can put everything else in order. However, the only difference from before is that God has moved to the top position of *our* priority list. The list is still *ours*. We remain at the bargaining table with God, deciding for ourselves what comes second, third, and so on. Our walk with God, even when He's in the number one position, continues to be just another area of life that competes to stay in first place.

The journey we're making becomes like a day at school in which we put in our time while anxiously looking forward to the ringing of the bell. While our mind is *sort of* focused on what the teacher is saying, our thoughts are racing ahead to what we'll do when the day is over. Our focus is divided; our mind is split. In the same way, in our journey with God we find our focus divided and our mind split. We see our allegiance divided between God's world and our own comfortable and familiar world in which we still "take care of ourselves." We end up having a civil war within us. We keep on promoting God to higher and higher offices, but *we* remain in the top position of the one doing the promoting. We find it more comfortable to continue committing certain things and situations and people to God rather than surrendering our life into God's hands. We find it safe to put God in first place on our priority list, as long as the priority list remains in our hands. While God is first on the list, He has not invaded the list itself. We're still at the controls.

As we experience the collision of our world and God's world, our minds are split and our lives are divided. We keep trying to find ways to squeeze God into our world, and He just doesn't seem to fit! We feel as if we're suffering from some type of Christian schizophrenia or spiritual multiple personalities. Facing a great identity crisis, we begin to ask ourselves, "Who am I . . . *really?*" With our focus split, we feel like undercover Christians who wear the Christian costume for certain occasions only to hang it up and put on another costume for other occasions. Like a member of a military reserve unit, we put on our uniform for our time of duty and then return to everyday life for the rest of the week. We begin to think like part-time Christians.

Finally, we face the reality that God can't be reserved for just a portion of our life, not even the top portion. Finding a place to squeeze God in and make Him fit into our world doesn't change a thing. Adding God to our lineup just gives us another piece that we have to juggle. Suddenly we come to realize that maybe we've been asking the wrong question all along. Could it be that the question is *not* "What role does God play in *my* life?" Rather, could the ultimate question be "What role do I play in *God's* life?" Instead of bringing God into our world, God invites us into *His* world!

The Ultimate Question: What Role Do I Play in God's Life?

When confronted with the question "What role do I play in God's life?" we're often like the young person who desired to know God's will for his life and, deciding to help God speed up the process, wrote down every possible thing that God might want to do in his life. He assumed that He would tell him to stop when he got to the "right thing."

After completing a long list, the young man ran out of things to write down. In desperation he cried out, "God, I really do want Your will in my life; I've listed all the possibilities. Why won't You show me what it is?" Ready to throw away the paper in frustration, he began to realize that God was not wanting some "thing" on *his* list—He wanted the blank paper on which the list was written.

In the same way, as our relationship with God grows, we think about all the *things* in our life that we might offer. However, God invites us to hand over our lives in the form of a blank sheet of paper. God does not want so much to be "first place" on our priority list, but rather, He wants to invade and infiltrate our priority list so that it becomes His list, and our lives become *His.* Rather than penciling God into our own personal stories, God wants to write us into *His* story.

Jesus' disciples did not simply invite Jesus to come into their lives of fishing and tax collecting. When Jesus called His disciples, He invited them to leave their old worlds of fishing nets and tax booths to join Him in an entirely new world, a world called "the kingdom of God." Dropping their familiar nets and walking away from their comfortable tax booths, they ventured out to follow Jesus wherever He would lead them in *His* world. They did not simply believe that Jesus was a king and then continue to live in the same old world in which they had always been living. They entered into a whole new existence—they became citizens of an alternative Kingdom!

No doubt, making God "fit" into our own familiar world seems more secure than living life in *His* unfamiliar world. Relying on ourselves will always appear to be safer than living a life of trust in someone else. This false sense of security and comfort is often the reason we struggle to live in God's alternative Kingdom. However, rather than staying in our familiar world and handing parts of our lives over to God piece by piece, we're invited to leave behind our old world and embark on a journey in *God's* world. God invites us to join Him in *His* story and to discover a whole new identity there.

Perhaps one of the greatest challenges we face in our journey with God is to step *out* of the comfort zone of *our* familiar world, where we try to make God fit, and to step *into* God's world. Like our first leap into the swimming pool where our parent urges us to jump into his or her arms, we're apprehensive about leaving the security and safety of the familiar, solid ground. We wonder, "Can I *really* trust my mom [or dad] to catch me?" However, once we've jumped and found ourselves in our parent's arms, we never want to go back to standing and watching from the sidelines.

The same is true when God calls us out of the security of our own world and into His world. Only as we step out of the comfort zone of our familiar world and into God's alternative world can we know what it *really* means to be led, taught, and transformed by Him. The great leap into the arms of God is a leap of trust! But the God who calls us to trust Him completely is trustworthy and dependable.

The Heart of the Obstacles

After several months in his journey with God, Adam began to recognize a common thread that seemed to run through the obstacles he had faced. Whether it be looking for quick fixes and rapid remedies through a particular experience, mimicking a significant spiritual mentor, trying to measure up to Jesus as his model, or finding a way to "fit" God into his world, Adam noticed that he was always the one in control. Adam's trust for his relationship with God was not so much in God but in himself. He had come to depend upon his own strengths and abilities to change himself. His journey with God had become repeated attempts at fixing himself, copying somebody else's religion, trying harder to be like Jesus, and squeezing God into an important place in his life. The world in which Adam was living continued to be *Adam's world*, not *God's world!* While bringing God into his own world, Adam continued to be very much in charge of his own life. God was just a new main character in his life story.

As the world in which he had always lived continued to collide with the alternative kingdom of God, Adam began to question if anything had *really* even happened at camp the previous summer. In the same way, as these two worlds collide in our lives we might also ask, "So did nothing *really* happen in that prayer at the altar, at the camp, or in the morning devotional?" Indeed, something incredible *did* happen. God graciously invited you to begin the most amazing, dynamic journey that you could ever go on. And you took the first step into that journey. You became a citizen of and an active participant in the alternative kingdom of God!

Having stepped foot into God's kingdom, you will experience transformation in your life far beyond what you could ever imagine. However, it is God who called you. It is God who forgave you. It is God who set you apart— and now it is God who will transform you. As you journey with God in His presence and as you remain open to Him and trust Him, He will *continue* to work in your life. He *began* His work in you, and He will *continue* to do His work in you. No doubt about it—God transforms our minds and changes our lives. You have responded to and accepted God's amazing love. The adventure has just begun. It is now that amazing love that will take you into the future and that will do more in your life than you could ever ask or imagine.

Let's continue our journey now by looking at what it meant for Adam and what it means for us to be *participants* in this incredible *alternative* kingdom of God!

⚠ Reflecting on Our Journey with God

1. Can you recall a time when you tried to take matters into your own hands and take care of yourself—only to realize later that you needed an expert?

2. In what ways do we tend to squeeze Jesus into our own lives?

3. Why do we often find it easier to put Jesus at the top of our priority list rather than opening up our list to let Him invade it?

4. As you continue to journey with God, in what ways might He be challenging you to go on by participating in something bigger than yourself—His story—rather than making God fit into your own life story?

5. To explore further what the Bible says about living our lives and participating in the life of Jesus Christ, read John 15:1-11; Romans 8:5-11; 1 Corinthians 10:16-17; Galatians 5:16-25; Philippians 3:10-11; 1 John 4:13-21; and 2 Peter 1:3-11.

Part 2
Discovering Our Identity:
What *Really* Happened?

Participants in the Story of God: From the Balcony to the Stage

As Adam hung up the phone, he couldn't believe what he had just agreed to do. A year earlier, he said that he would never waste his money on that "tourist trap" again. But his buddies just had a good way of changing his mind; after all, he didn't have anything else planned. Several of his friends in the youth group were going to see what the local amusement park advertised every Christmas as "the world's largest Nativity scene." Even though he had gone with his family last year, he decided to go again this year with his friends.

As he reluctantly got dressed, Adam thought back to last year's visit. His family had decided to have one of those "family nights out." As they got to the ticket counter, all of them were shocked—15 dollars per person seemed awfully steep. After debating whether or not to go in, they decided that since they had come this far, they might as well see what all the fuss was about. As they went through the gate, Adam exclaimed, "This thing better be worth it—I could have hit a lot of video games for this much!" As soon as they got inside the park, Adam noticed that all of the "good rides" were closed. Only the little kids' rides and the antique merry-go-round were running.

After getting some hot chocolate, Adam's family followed the arrows to "the world's largest Nativity scene." They ended up at the park's mammoth performance hall. Going through the massive glass doors, Adam could hear a recording of "The Hallelujah Chorus" being played inside the auditorium. As they walked into the auditorium, the sight was overwhelming! A larger-than-life-size Nativity scene of plaster figurines was spread clear across the auditorium's huge stage. Every member of the Christmas cast was present. Mary and Joseph were at center stage. Baby Jesus was tucked in between them. At the far right end of the stage were at least half a dozen shepherds with a couple dozen sheep. At the opposite end of the stage were the wise men with gifts in hand. Donkeys, cows, and camels were scattered throughout the stage. Hanging from the stage ceiling were angels with their wings stretched out and with trumpets raised to their mouths.

For a couple of minutes, the whole family silently gazed at the scene in amazement. Even Adam was speechless! A brief silence followed "The Hallelujah Chorus." Then the same song started right back up. Adam looked over at his mom as she shrugged her shoulders. His dad broke the silence by saying, "So you think that's all there is?" After a couple more minutes, the family made their way out of the performance hall. On the way out, Alyssa exclaimed, "I can't believe it! It was beautiful, but 15 dollars to stand in front of a Nativity scene for five minutes and look at a bunch of statues from a distance is kind of drastic!"

Adam added, "I wouldn't call it 'drastic.' I'd call it a rip-off!" On their way out of the park, the family agreed that this would be the last time they would visit this "attraction."

Now, one year later, Adam couldn't believe that he had agreed to go again. He thought that he had learned his lesson last year. But his friends had some two-for-one coupons, and there wasn't anything else to do anyway. Also, he had heard that a huge ice-skating rink had been added.

As soon as the group got to the park, Adam led the way to the performance hall. He thought he might as well get the viewing over with and get on to better things like skating. As he entered the auditorium, he couldn't believe the way everything had changed. The stage that last year held all the figures was now solid ice, with at least a couple hundred people skating on it. His first thought was that the "world's largest Nativity scene" had come to life with ice-skates on each character. Although he wanted to go ahead and join everybody else on the ice, he decided to join a couple of his friends in tracking down where the Nativity scene had been moved.

After checking out a couple of the smaller auditoriums, Adam and his friends stumbled upon the most amazing sight right in the middle of the park. Adam couldn't believe how things had changed this year. The characters were still the same; however, where he now stood made them look completely different. There were no seats for spectators. There was no stage for the figures. The metal bar that had separated the Nativity scene from the onlookers was gone. Adam and his friends were able to walk right up to each one of the characters. They entered right into the middle of the Nativity scene as if they also were characters themselves. Adam first went and stood alongside Mary. Looking into Baby Jesus' face from Mary's perspective was awesome. Moving over to the shepherds, Adam felt as if he were actually one of them. On his way over to the wise men, he crossed under several angels. Finding his place among the wise men, Adam imagined what it must have been like to bring a gift to this baby King. Everything about the Nativity scene was so different this year. Adam exclaimed to his friends who were with him, "Man! This is really cool. Last year my family and I stood up in the balcony way far away from the stage. We saw everything from a distance. We were just spectators. This year, I feel like I'm a character in the story myself. It seems like we're as much participants in the birth story of Jesus as the shepherds, the wise men, and the angels."

It's amazing how much the view changes when you get out of the balcony and onto the stage. It's like a whole new world to go from being a *spectator* to being a *participant*.

Out of the Spectators' Balcony and onto the Stage

Spectator or participant? The choice really does make a huge difference in everything we do in life. It is exciting to *watch* a football game in which the wide receiver makes the winning touchdown by running 65 yards in the final seconds. However, it is entirely different to actually *be* the quarterback who throws the winning pass or the wide receiver who makes the touchdown. It is inspiring to *attend* a performance by an incredible orchestra. But it is a whole other experience to *be* a member of the band itself. It is motivating to *see* your sister or brother cross the platform and receive a diploma. But it's an entirely different matter when you *are* the one who's graduating. "Looking on" is not all that bad, but if you're ever going to experience the dynamic adventures of life, there comes a time to get out of the spectators' balcony and on to the playing field of life!

When Adam returned home that night from the amusement park, he kept being reminded how drastically different things were at the Nativity scene this year. The difference was not the characters in the scene; the difference was where he stood in relationship to the scene. Suddenly he began to realize what an incredible change had taken place in his walk with God since last year. He had come out of the spectators' balcony and had set foot on the stage of God's incredible drama. What a huge difference there was between *watching* what God was doing in other people's lives and *participating* in what God was doing! What an amazing contrast between having a remote, static religion in which he was simply an onlooker and actively joining in a journey with God and with members of God's family! What an incredible difference there was between being a "religious" person who could talk about what God did several thousand years ago and being in a dynamic relationship with a God who was doing things in the present! More than agreeing to follow a list of rules, memorize special lines, or attend certain meetings, Adam had become an *active participant* in the story of God.

Participants in God's Story, Not Our Own

To be an *active participant* in the story of God means that the little stories of our individual lives are swallowed up into something so much bigger than just us. We become a part of something greater than ourselves. Rather than our adding God to the cast of characters in *our* own little stories, God allows us to become characters in the greatest story of all time: His story! Rather than our *adding* God on to our social, academic, physical, and emotional life, God allows our lives as a whole to become a part of something that stretches so far beyond us—His story. Rather than our participating in our favorite religious system, a good moral cause, a trustworthy political movement, or an effective social program, God allows us to become a part of something that has been going on from the very beginning of time—His story.

As we enter into a trusting relationship with God, we discover that we are connected to something grander, deeper, and wider than our own individual lives. Millions of people who have come before us, who are scattered all over the globe today, and who will come after us are also a part of the story of God. We are directly related to the great heroes and heroines of the Bible and of the Christian Church. The list of names could go on forever: Abraham, Sarah, Moses, Miriam, David, Deborah, Jeremiah, Hannah, Elijah, Esther, Peter, Mary, Paul, Martha, Ignatius, Mary Magdalene, Augustine, Theresa of Avila, William Tyndale, Martin Luther, John Wesley, William Carey, Dietrich Bonhoeffer, Mother Teresa. They are *all* our ancestors. We have been added to the family tree, and we belong to that family tree as much as any of them do!

We are part of an amazingly diverse family scattered throughout the world. As participants in the story of God, we never make this journey alone. We are never the only one who has responded to God's invitation to become a part of His story. We have brothers and sisters in every corner of the earth. They represent all ages, they speak different languages, they belong to different races and cultures, they carry out different customs, they worship in different ways, but they all participate in the same story of God in which we participate. Indeed, we are participants in something that is great!

We are no longer religious spectators who watch God work from a distance. God is no longer a remote power who worked thousands of years ago or is limited to a few people today. We can give up the game of squeezing God into *our* world, because God invites us to be swallowed up in *His* world. We can stop trying to pencil in God in the little book of our lives, because God is writing us in to His book. God is not a character in our story; we are characters in *His* story. What a reason for celebration! We have been invited to leave the spectators' balcony and the sidelines to enter the arena of God's story.

Participants in an Amazing Plot

Throughout human history, God has been calling people regardless of their age, gender, culture, race, or background to join Him in an incredible plot. God has never been into carrying out His plot by making long-distance phone calls or by zapping the world with divine lightning bolts. Instead, He uses common, ordinary people in His story. He looks for people just like us who are willing to get onto the stage with Him and join Him in what He's doing. So if we really are among the many characters in God's story, what *is* His plot? What in the world is God trying to do?

Make no mistake about it—God is doing a whole lot more than making the world a better place in which to live. He is involved in something so much bigger than setting up a moral system of rules for human beings to carry out. He is building something so much more meaningful than an exclusive social club where insiders can find new friends. God has a much greater concern than simply getting us into heaven. What, then, is He doing?

God is not a remote, long-distance ruler who gets His kicks seeing how well we can measure up to His commands. Rather, God is a loving Creator who desires an intimate, mutual relationship with all of humanity. In this relationship, God desires to be the One who freely provides life and for us to respond by loving and trusting Him completely. Therefore, the plot of God's story is simply God's taking the initiative to restore this trusting relationship between himself and the human race whom He created and loves so deeply.

In the plot of God's story, God desires relationship over religion, trust over anxiety, shared life over independence, and giving over receiving. God's desire for this relationship with humanity goes so deep that rather than inviting us to come to where He is, *He* comes to where *we* are. Rather than restoring this relationship by telling us that we first must straighten up our acts and love Him, He first loved us by living among us and by giving up His life for us. The restored relationship that God desires to have with humanity comes completely from *God's* initiative. Nothing that we could give, perform, or accomplish could ever even begin to restore that relationship. We simply trust that what God has freely done was enough to restore that relationship, receive what God has freely done, and continue to live our lives according to what He has freely done.

What an incredible plot! But what makes it even more amazing is that we are not watching it from a distance. Like Adam and his friends in "the world's largest Nativity scene," we have left the spectators' balcony and have become active participants in God's drama of restored relationship. As our relationships with God are restored, we discover that we have become a part of a community that Jesus himself established, the Church. We join this community as it celebrates, participates in, and lives out what God is doing in His world. We discover that we have truly become participants in an *alternative* world, the *alternative kingdom of God!*

⚠ Reflecting on Our Journey with God

1. What are some activities in everyday life in which you participate? What are some activities in which you're a spectator? What difference does it make as to whether we're participants or spectators?

2. In our journey with God, why might we tend to stand on the sidelines and be spectators?

3. Where do you see yourself fitting as a character in God's story? Who are some of the characters in God's story (both past and present) with whom you particularly identify?

4. In the journey you're making with God, how might you go on by coming down from the spectators' balcony and discovering your active role in God's drama?

5. To further explore what the Bible says about our participation in God's story and in His community, read Romans 12:3-8; 1 Corinthians 12:4-31; 2 Corinthians 5:16—6:1; Ephesians 2:11-22; Hebrews 4:14-16; 11:1—12:2.

Let the same mind be in you
that was in Christ Jesus.
—Philippians 2:5

Living in the Alternative Kingdom

As the Christmas season arrived, family members from all over the country began to invade the Robertson house. With the exception of losing his bedroom to Grandma for a week and not being able to eat with the grownups, Adam always looked forward to this exciting time of the year.

A couple of days before Christmas, Alyssa and Adam had the "privilege" of entertaining their two younger cousins, eight-year-old Andrew and six-year-old Jeff, while the grown-ups went out to do some last-minute shopping. Adam and Alyssa knew that an afternoon with their cousins would definitely not be boring. After discussing just what they should do for a whole afternoon with Andrew and Jeff, they decided to take them downtown to visit what always seemed to be a favorite. As soon as the car pulled into the parking space downtown, Andrew and Jeff were off and running. After crossing four lanes of two-way traffic, they all arrived at their destination.

The bright neon sign that hung overhead read "LaserWorld." The building was a renovated three-story apartment complex, equipped with secret passages, mirrors, ramps, and strobe lights.

Once inside LaserWorld, each player choose a code name. Alyssa and Adam were not surprised by the names their cousins selected. Wanting to register fear in front of all the other players, Andrew chose "The Punisher" for his code name, and Jeff decided on "The Enforcer." When the time came for the game to begin, the players were taken into a small, dark room. With black lights lining the ceiling, neon paint splattered all over the walls gave off a bright glow. After the players had put on their packs of bright flashing lights, the guy in charge began to give instructions. He introduced himself to the players as "The Marshall." Asking the 30 people crowded in the room to raise their laser pistols in the air, "The Marshall" had everyone repeat the Laser Oath: "I will not run. I will not push. I will not spit gum on the floor. I will not use bad language. I will play hard, play tough, and play to win."

After giving final instructions, "The Marshall" concluded by saying, "Now many of you have played laser tag at other places, but you've never played the game quite like it's played at LaserWorld. In other games, you were probably on a team working with other people; that is *not* the way the game works at LaserWorld. Here the number one rule is every person for himself or herself." The crowd broke out in cheers and applause. The thought of 30 lone rangers in rapid pursuit of each other was stirring up the adrenaline. Pointing to what looked like a garage door, "The Marshall" continued, "In a few minutes, you'll see this door begin to rise. As the door rises, you'll see smoke and flashing lights; you'll hear music and a steady beat. Whatever you do, don't forget the first rule of the game: Every person for himself and herself! In this world, your friends are your enemies. All of you are after the same prize, and there are no points for second place."

As the garage door began to rise, smoke poured out, bright lights flashed, and music blared out from the speakers. It seemed like a force of suction pulled the first 20 soldiers right into the three-story war zone. The players started screaming, yelling, and running. The other players piled in right behind.

Only Alyssa, Adam, and their cousins remained. Andrew was eagerly waiting to go rush in. However, Jeff began to panic. When Adam asked him what was going on, Jeff responded, "Adam! I've never played the game this way. Every time I've played, I've been on a team. Why do they make us play by ourselves? Why can't you, me, Andrew, and Alyssa team up against everybody else? We wouldn't even have to tell anybody."

Overhearing Jeff, Andrew responded, "Get with the program, Man. You heard what the guy said—'There are no teams in this game. It's every man and every woman for himself and herself.' Grow up, Jeff. In this game you play hard, you play tough, and you play to win—by yourself! This is the *real* world we're talking about, Man."

His heart racing, Jeff replied, "But it doesn't *have* to be that way. There *is* another way. We don't *have* to play according to those rules." Refusing to take Jeff's nonsense anymore, Andrew ran through the door and into the war zone. Following closely behind Andrew, Jeff continued, "Adam, it really doesn't *have* to be that way. There *is* another way. Together—" The suction of the war zone behind the garage door seemed to swallow Jeff right in with everybody else. In less than a minute, he was playing just like everybody else—according to the rules of the real world—*by himself.*

At the end of the day, Adam thought about his afternoon at LaserWorld. He realized how much the "real world" in which he was living every day of his life was like the war zone that had inhaled all of them. It was a world that says, "If you're going to win, it's up to you. There are no teams; it's every person for himself or herself. Play hard, play tough, and play to win!" It's a world that focuses on our own ability to succeed. When the scorecard of life is printed up in this *real world,* all that really matters is how well you have achieved.

The more Adam thought about it, the more he continued to hear his youngest cousin's words: "It doesn't *have* to be that way—there *is* another way." Adam began to think that Jeff's words might *really* be true. Could it be that in life there really is a whole other way? What if there is a world in direct contrast to what everybody else calls the *real world?* Could it be that this other world is what some people call the kingdom of God? Adam began to realize that as a *participant* in God's story, he was actually a citizen of this "other world"—this *alternative* kingdom of God.

An *Alternative* Kingdom?

So what is it that makes God's world so *alternative?* This alternative Kingdom is definitely not some mystical place where Christians run for shelter from the everyday "real world." Nor is it located outside the "real world" of everyday life. In no way did Jesus look at the chaotic darkness of our "LaserWorld," see it as beyond repair, and create a safe environment to which we could run and hide. He did not come to take us out of the slums of this "real world" to put us in a safe shelter outside of town. In fact, participants in God's alternative kingdom are never alienated from the pain, brokenness, and sin of the real world. This Kingdom is not alternative, because it is located *outside* the real world of everyday life.

Actually God's *alternative* kingdom makes sense only in the middle of *real*, everyday life. Just as a streetlight on a dark, foggy night stands out in the thick darkness, this *alternative* world stands out from the world in which it finds itself. It is different and peculiar. The contrast between the streetlight and the foggy darkness has nothing to do with the metal covering or the rusted pole of the light, but it has everything to do with the light that shines *from within*. In the same way, what makes God's *alternative* kingdom different from the world in which we live is *not* first the things we do, the places we go, the way we speak, or how we look. What makes God's world *alternative* starts from *within*. The heart of the difference in this Kingdom is a transformed way of thinking and of seeing the world around us. As we become citizens of this alternative world, we are not given a new place to live, but we are given a new mind-set. We are not taken *out of* our everyday world, but we are given a new set of lenses through which we can see our everyday world. To live in this Kingdom is to have an *alternative* way of thinking and an *alternative* way of seeing.

An Alternative Way of "Thinking"— the Mind of Christ

So what kind of change takes place in our mind as we live in this alternative Kingdom? Ultimately, our minds are being transformed into the very mind of Jesus Christ. Beyond the question of what Jesus would do, where He would go, and what He would say, the heart of this alternative Kingdom is *first* "How does Jesus think? What is the mind of Christ?"

No doubt, something about Jesus was radically *alternative* from everybody around Him, including the religious people. Regardless of age, status, or background, all the people knew that Jesus accepted them where they were. While Jesus lived with common people, spoke the common language, and participated in common activities, he had a very uncommon way of acting. He just seemed to radiate light in the thick darkness. While His actions were holy, He never made himself or his actions the center of attention. He performed good deeds, but not for the applause of people. He was definitely a contrast to the *real world* in which He lived.

However, what made Jesus so different went much deeper than the way He acted. Although His deeds were radically *alternative,* at the heart of the difference was a radically *alternative* way of *thinking.* The way He thought was *alternative* in every way imaginable; His thoughts literally turned the world upside down. Jesus spoke about a world that seemed strange and foreign to many people. In Jesus' way of thinking, the weak were strong, the last were first, outsiders were insiders, the least were greatest, outcasts were accepted, the poor were rich, and dead people lived again! No doubt, as people imagined this *alternative* Kingdom about which Jesus spoke, many persons had to become hopeful. What if the powerless really *were* powerful? What if the poor beggars really *were* rich? What if our place in line was not determined by our performance or accomplishments? However, once the *real world* of "Play hard, play tough, play to win" and "Every person for himself or herself" set back in, most people concluded that Jesus was just a hopeful dreamer. Passing a hungry beggar or a greedy tax collector, they likely thought, "His dream is noble, but it's so far from the *real world.* In the *real world* the rich will always be powerful and will always use their power to get ahead. In the *real world* the hungry and thirsty will always go to sleep empty and unsatisfied. In the *real world* each person is a lone ranger pushing to the top of the hill." Could Jesus not see the "real world"? Was He really that out of touch with reality? To hear Jesus talk about this *alternative* Kingdom was like standing at the North Pole and hearing someone talk about the warm beaches of Florida. The world described by Jesus was just too foreign, too strange, too distant, and too *alternative*. This world was nowhere to be seen.

Other people who really wanted to believe in what Jesus was saying might have thought that this alternative Kingdom was something in the distant future. Seeing the dividing lines between first and last, rich and poor, strong and weak in the present *real world*, they often asked, "So when does this alternative Kingdom begin?" However, Jesus made it clear that this Kingdom was not simply a future *place* of great rewards, magnificent mansions, and pearly gates. This Kingdom was not something about which a person would say, "Here it is" or "There it is." Instead, this Kingdom was a whole new *way of thinking*. This radically different way of thinking for Jesus was not so much *what* Jesus saw, but *how* He saw it. He saw life through a radically different set of lenses. Not only did Jesus see things differently—He offered the same set of lenses to those people who followed Him. He offered a whole new way of seeing reality.

An Alternative Way of Seeing:
Life from a New Perspective

Jesus continues to invite the persons who follow Him to view life through "alternative Kingdom lenses." Most of us are familiar with and often live by the real-world slogan of "If it's going to be, it's up to me." We live as if life really is dependent upon us. However, we're invited to see life and then live it through an entirely different set of lenses. *God* provides, not us! This vision of life requires a radical dependency on someone *outside* of ourselves. In Jesus' prayer of this alternative Kingdom, the Lord's Prayer, our total dependency upon God is expressed in phrases like *"Give* us . . . bread," *"Forgive* us our debts [sins]," and *"Rescue* us from . . . evil." As citizens of God's alternative kingdom, we realize that things like nourishment, forgiveness, and security are ultimately outside of ourselves; our dependence and trust is in God.

So how do we respond to this Kingdom? Oftentimes with one foot in God's alternative world and the other foot remaining in our everyday *real* world, we try to live in both. We think, "I'll provide until I can provide no more, then I'll allow God to provide." However, if we're ever truly to discover our full citizenship in God's alternative kingdom, our attempts to be self-sufficient and self-reliant will finally be swallowed up by the Kingdom where God is *really* God. Until our lives are surrendered into God's alternative kingdom, our journey with Him is like neither that of an eagle that soars majestically over the cares of the "real world" nor that of an ostrich that possesses the wings but is never even lifted off of the ground. Our journey will be more like that of a hen that will occasionally lift off the ground but never for any length of time. While we possess the wings, we never understand where they were meant to take us. We find ourselves getting a taste of life in God's alternative kingdom, only to fall back into the real world of "If it's going to be, it's up to me." We find our lives divided, one foot in the kingdom of God and the other foot in the world of self-sufficiency and self-reliance.

As we trust God to be the provider of *all* our life, we discover what it means for us to be citizens in this alternative Kingdom. We are no longer citizens of that world where we provide and where it's "Every person for himself and herself." Living in this Kingdom, our minds are changed in the way we view life. We begin to think the way Jesus thinks, and we begin to see the way Jesus sees. As God transforms us from within, we begin to view life from an entirely different perspective, the perspective of His alternative kingdom. We no longer see life as dependent upon us. We begin to see other people from this perspective as well, the way Jesus saw them. Rather than looking with our eyes for performance, achievement, and accomplishment, we look with our hearts— hearts of love, acceptance, and forgiveness.

Viewing Life from the *Alternative* Perspective

All of us are intimately familiar with the real-world question of "What can I do?" "What can I accomplish?" or "How can I achieve?" In our real world of living life as if it were up to us, Jesus invites us to view life from an alternative perspective, one of neediness, emptiness, and helplessness.

An event in Jesus' life helps us see this. It is described in Luke 10:25-29. One day a lawyer asked Jesus just what it was that *he himself* needed to do to be a part of the kingdom of God. His question reflects the *real world* perspective of personal achievement and self-sufficiency. He said, "What do *I need to do* to have eternal life?"

Jesus responded, "You're a lawyer; what does the law say?"

The lawyer replied, "Love the Lord your God with all your heart, soul, and strength; and love your neighbor as yourself."

"Very good," Jesus replied. "Do this, and you will have life."

As he turned to walk away, the lawyer asked, "So, who is my neighbor?" In other words, "How far down the totem pole of people does my love have to reach?"

Living in the everyday, real world, the lawyer's focus continued to be upon what he could *do*. However, Jesus now provides the lawyer an *alternative* perspective from which to view life. Taking the man on a brief journey, it is as if Jesus offers the man a pair of 3-D lenses to see the world as he had never seen it before.

Jesus tells a story (Luke 10:30-37) about a man traveling down a busy road. The man is attacked and left to die in a ditch. With the hope of help quickly fading, a religious leader passes by. What incredible timing! But for whatever reason, he doesn't stop. A second religious leader passes by, but the response is the same. As the sun sets, the man in the ditch closes his eyes for what might be the last time. Suddenly, he's awakened by a man who knows what it's like to live in the ditches of society. The man is a Samaritan, a social and religious outcast. Reaching down into the ditch, the Samaritan pulls the wounded man up into his arms and rescues him. Jesus concludes the story by asking the lawyer, "Now which one of these persons was the neighbor?"

As the lawyer stands listening to Jesus, the world that he had so carefully built begins to crumble. Jesus has not responded as the lawyer expected Him to. The lawyer has always seen himself as the one passing by; his job is to help the person in the ditch. From the perspective of strength, ability, and high accomplishments, his question to Jesus is basically "Now who in the ditch is my neighbor that I should help him?" However, in Jesus' question to the lawyer, He does not place the lawyer in the position of strong people who can help the person in need. Rather, He places the lawyer in the position of the guy in the ditch. Jesus turns the lawyer's world upside down by providing an alternative perspective—a view of life *from the ditch!* Instead of offering the lawyer an opportunity to accomplish and perform by helping the people in the ditch, Jesus responds by implying, "So, if you're the guy stranded in the ditch waiting to die, which of these persons is your neighbor?" In this story, Jesus offers not only the lawyer but all of us an alternative perspective to view life. From this perspective, Jesus provides us with a new way of thinking and a new way of seeing life.

As good as it is to help the person in the ditch, the starting point in God's alternative kingdom is to view life from the dependent, helpless, and hopeful perspective of the ditch. Only after we see life from the helplessness of the ditch can we extend our hand to others in it. We give because we have first been given. We love because we have first been loved.

Life in God's alternative kingdom begins when we see ourselves from the ditch, when we can admit our own helplessness and our dependency on One outside of ourselves. From the perspective of the ditch, we can begin to see and think in the radically alternative way of Christ. This mind-set is ultimately a radical dependency upon God, where God alone is provider, and not us. In this Kingdom we come to recognize and celebrate that we were never created as gods, we aren't gods now, and we never will be gods. God is God, and we aren't! To accept this fact, to rest in this fact, and to celebrate this fact is to step foot into the alternative world of radical trust in God. From this perspective, the way we see life and the way we think are radically transformed.

Adam and Alyssa's cousin really was right: "It doesn't *have* to be that way. There *is* another way. Together . . ." This alternative kingdom of God is that "other way" in which it's no longer "play tough, play hard, and play to win." It's a life lived "together"—a life of trust in God.

Reflecting on Our Journey with God

1. Where in everyday life do we see and hear the following mottoes?

  a. If it's going to be, it's up to me.

  b. Play hard, play tough, and play to win.

  c. It's every person for himself or herself.

2. In what ways does God's alternative kingdom turn the real world of everyday life upside down? How does living in God's alternative kingdom make us aliens and strangers in our everyday world?

3. How is God's alternative kingdom first a change in the way we think and see?

4. In your journey with God, how is He challenging you to go on by living life in His alternative kingdom and by seeing life from the perspective of the person in the ditch?

5. To further explore what the Bible says about living in the everyday real world while having our citizenship in God's alternative kingdom, read Deuteronomy 12:29-32; Joshua 24:14-18; 1 Kings 18:20-39; Matthew 6:19-24; Mark 10:35-45; John 15:18-26; 17:6-19; Romans 12:1-2; Ephesians 6:10-17; Hebrews 11:13-16; and 1 John 2:15-25.

By grace you have been saved through faith, and this is not your own doing; it is the gift of God—not the result of works, so that no one may boast.

—Ephesians 2:8-9

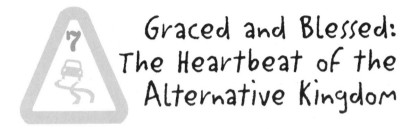

Graced and Blessed: The Heartbeat of the Alternative Kingdom

As Adam was coming to understand what it meant for him to be a participant in God's alternative kingdom, the words of his cousin at LaserWorld kept being replayed in his mind: "It doesn't have to be that way—there *is* another way!" As a citizen of God's "alternative kingdom," Adam realized that he was still living in what his friends called the real world, but his mind was being shaped by a whole other world. Day by day, his whole understanding of life was changing. In this other Kingdom, life was not based on the slogan "If it's going to be, it's up to me." There really *was* another way. In this alternative kingdom of God, everything was turned upside down. Adam began to wonder what was at the heart of it that turned everything upside down. How was serving considered to be true greatness? What made the least actually the first? Why were empty people filled? How was strength found in weakness? Why is real life found when the attempt to rescue life is given up?

Adam was soon to discover the heartbeat of his new identity in this alternative kingdom of God. Early one morning Alyssa, who was still home for Christmas break, invited Adam to go along with her for a quick morning run. They could not have asked for a better morning—the sun was shining and a gentle morning breeze was blowing. As they made their way down a hill, they saw a group of elementary school kids goofing off, playing tag, and joking around as they waited for the school bus. Coming down the hill just ahead of them was a little girl at least six inches shorter than the other kids. Wearing an oversized green plastic rain jacket, she was carrying an umbrella under one arm and a stack of books under the other arm. In one hand she had a lunch sack; in the other hand she had a huge drawing pad and a box of crayons.

As the little girl came running toward the other kids, the kids at the stop began a chant with which they seemed to be very familiar. The words echoed throughout the neighborhood: "Here comes the *bus reject!* Look at the *bus reject!* We don't like *bus rejects* around here. You can smell the *bus reject* all the way down here. Get to the back of the line, you *bus reject!*" Stopping dead in their tracks, Adam and Alyssa could not believe what they were hearing. As the little girl stepped into the crowd of kids, the chant got louder and more intense.

Turning to Adam, Alyssa said, "If that were me, I'd run back home and tell Mom that I was sick."

Adam responded, "Not me! I'd show them that I wasn't a bus reject."

"But look at her, Adam," Alyssa said. "Just look at her!"

What Alyssa and Adam saw was amazing. As she stood at the back of the line, the little girl's brown eyes danced like diamonds. A beautiful smile covered her face. Shrugging his shoulders and shaking his head, Adam said, "She must not be able to understand what they're saying. Hey—let's go!"

As they began to jog up the next hill, Alyssa said to Adam, "Do you think she really heard what they were saying?"

"She had to," Adam responded.

"But, Adam, did you see the way her eyes sparkled? And that smile on her face seemed real. It was like her mind was focused on a whole other world!"

As Adam and Alyssa reached the top of the hill, there stood a woman right in the middle of the road. Adam looked over at Alyssa and said, "Must be *Big Mama.*" The woman looked like a grown-up version of the "bus reject." With an umbrella under an arm, magazines under the other arm, a lunch pail in one hand, and a writing pad in the other hand, she was even wearing a green plastic rain jacket. Standing in the middle of the road, she raised her hand to her lips, blew a kiss, and waved down the hill. Looking over at Alyssa, Adam said, "She's not blowing those kisses at *me,* is she?"

Alyssa responded, "In your dreams!"

As they laughed, Adam and Alyssa knew exactly where the morning breeze was taking those kisses. Still faintly hearing the morning chant as it echoed through the neighborhood, they looked behind them. At the bottom of the hill, they saw the form of the little girl in the back of the line with a green plastic rain jacket; she was blowing kisses up the hill and waving. They looked ahead, and there was her mother—blowing kisses and waving.

Before going on with their jog, Adam said, "Man! We're caught in the crossfire."

Alyssa responded, "Yeah! But now I think we know why that little girl's eyes were so bright and why her smile was so real. Even though she heard the chant of the other kids, her identity isn't based on those kids' ridicule and rejection. Her mind's focused on a whole other world—she finds who she is in the world of her mother."

Adam exclaimed, "Alyssa, you've got it! You've got it!"

Glancing over at Adam with a puzzled look, Alyssa responded, "I've got *what?* What are you talking about?"

"You've got it! That's it! It's not that the girl didn't hear the chants; instead, those chants did *not* shape who she was. Her identity was shaped by her mother's love, acceptance, and forgiveness. Alyssa, I really see for the first time what happened to me last summer. I stepped *out of* a world of morning chants where my identity is based upon performance, achievements, and accomplishments. I stepped *into* a world where my identity is based upon love, acceptance, and forgiveness. As I find my identity in that world, I no longer have to spend my life *proving* myself to other people or to God in order to be accepted. I already am accepted and loved for who I am, not for how well I can perform or for how successful I am in certain activities. I'm living life, finding identity, and seeing everything around me in *that* world."

Alyssa responded, "You know, Adam, you *really* are beginning to see what's now happening to you. You became a participant in God's alternative *world of grace,* and you now live in that world!"

God's Alternative World of Grace

Adam was beginning to see the heartbeat of this alternative Kingdom where strength was found in weakness and where greatness was in being least. He was discovering why life was found by giving up the search to make his life secure. There is not anything "magical" about being weak or least or last. In our emptiness, there's nothing we can do in our power to make life happen. In this Kingdom, if we have life at all, it will not depend upon our being the strongest, the best, or the first. If life is not up to us, then our dependency is not based upon our performance. Our trust is not based upon our accomplishments. And our security is not based upon what we can accumulate and earn. Being weak and helpless, we find that our dependency, our trust, and our security is in Someone *outside of ourselves*. That Someone is God.

Suddenly Adam was understanding why God's world of grace is filled with "bus rejects" who are accepted, forgiven, and called by God. God's grace made the difference in their lives, not their own strengths or abilities. Powerless and insignificant people who appear unqualified to everyone else become the great characters of God's story. These persons never won their positions through competitions. To have looked at them, no one would ever have guessed that they could do the job.

Thinking about the persons who make up God's story is like walking through a museum of "bus rejects." In spite of many weaknesses, Sarah and Abraham became the ancestors of a great nation. Although he struggled to get a word out of his mouth, Moses became a great leader. A group of simple, untrained, and disorganized slaves defeated the world power. Even though he was the youngest of his family and was a simple shepherd, David became a great king of Israel. Although he was young and easily intimidated, Jeremiah was called by God to proclaim a bold message. In spite of her age and fear, Mary gave birth to the Savior of all humanity. While they were at the bottom of the social and religious totem pole, the shepherds were the first to hear and tell the good news of Jesus' birth. Although he was a simple fisherman and often a coward, Peter became the bold leader of the Christian Church.

The cast of characters goes on and on. Everywhere we turn in God's story, we encounter people who are the least likely candidates according to our world's standards. But we're talking about another world, God's alternative kingdom. In this Kingdom, God calls, prepares, and journeys with weak and frail people who cannot make it on their own performance, accomplishments, and outward qualities. Yet He looks at us and says, "You're the one, the one I love, accept, forgive, and call!" What kind of world is this? It's God's alternative world of grace.

One other very important set of characters in God's story is a group of people Jesus spent a lot of time with—sinners! When it came to serving God, these people were the ultimate "rejects." They were totally weak, helpless, and frail. They had no religious system that they could follow in order to please God. The kind of life they lived separated them completely from God and from religion. They had no sacrifices to make, no gifts to bring, no offerings to give, no songs to sing, and no rules to keep. All they had was the repulsive and ugly stuff of life, stuff like weakness, sickness, powerlessness, rejection, and sin. But these were the people Jesus came to and said, "I love you! I accept you! I forgive you!"

What is grace? Grace is God's choice of you before you could ever perform, accomplish, or achieve anything. Grace is God's love for you before you could ever imagine loving Him. Grace is God's acceptance of you before you could ever make yourself acceptable. Grace is God's leaning toward you before you ever had the strength to lean toward Him. Grace is God's forgiveness of *all* your disobedient acts before you could do anything to earn His forgiveness. Grace is God's power to change your life before you could ever begin a program of self-helps and spiritual makeovers. Grace is God's opening up the path to journey with Him forever before you ever knew there was a path.

Grace-Shaped Identity

As we come to live in God's alternative world of grace, an incredible change takes place in our lives. It goes much deeper than the way we feel. No doubt, when we realize the amazing truth of God's grace, our feelings and emotions are often affected. We all have different ways of feeling deep inside, and we have different ways of expressing those feelings on the outside. However, feelings and emotions come and go. Because we sometimes confuse our feelings as the presence or absence of God's grace, if we aren't experiencing a "spiritual high," we conclude that something must be wrong in our walk with God. However, the way we feel or don't feel and the way we express or don't express those feelings at a certain moment does not measure the power of God's grace in our lives. The change that God's grace makes in our lives goes deeper than our feelings.

In the same way, the change that God's grace makes in our lives goes much deeper than our personal determination to improve our behavior. Make no mistake about it—when God's grace explodes into our lives, the way we live our lives is radically affected. However, it brings a change to something that lies *behind* our conduct. Sometimes we accept God's grace in our lives only to turn right around and make a list of the things we need to do and another list of the things we should not do. As we make those lists, we fail to stop long enough to think about *why* certain changes need to happen. Changes in the way we live our lives are *not* the starting point of our walk with God; they are the *result* of a much deeper change that has first taken place. That change is a change in our identity—who we are. Our lifestyle is the expression of *who we are.*

More than a change in the way we feel or the way we act, when we accept the grace of God into our lives, our *identity* is transformed! We are no longer who we were. The understanding we have of life, God, other people, and ourselves is changed. Our old identity is gone, and we receive a new identity. And God is the One who makes the identity transformation.

What an incredible new identity we're given! No longer do we have a broken relationship with God, but God *really does* put us into a right relationship with Him. He doesn't simply close His eyes and "pretend" that we're forgiven; He really *does* forgive us! Our past is most definitely in the past, and we can leave it there—because God leaves it there. In this identity change, it's as if God begins creation all over again in our lives. He molds us as He breathes life into us moment by moment. As God shapes us into the likeness of Jesus, we come to discover what it means to be a human being at his or her very best. As we are given a whole new identity, we become a part of a huge family in which we become sons and daughters who are "at home" living in God's presence and living with each other. We discover that we have more brothers and sisters than we ever dreamed of having.

What a remarkable identity transformation—we're brought into a right relationship, we're given a brand-new life, and we're adopted into a huge family! But this identity change does not take place by reforming our ways, trying a little harder, or following a few self-help steps. Only God's grace brings about the identity change. Our identity rests on being the *graced, blessed, gifted children of God.* As we live out of our grace-shaped identity, our dependence is no longer upon our own strengths, abilities, or religious achievements. Life is no longer "up to us" and our performance. Instead, it's a gift for which we could never accomplish enough to deserve it.

In the same way that the "bus reject's" identity was based on the world of her mother's love rather than the performance-ruled world of the kids at the bottom of the hill, our identity is no longer based upon proving ourselves and earning rewards. It's now found in a love of which we're not worthy, in a forgiveness that we never had coming, and in an acceptance that we could never earn. In the world of God's grace, life is a gift, not an accomplishment.

Daily Life in the World of Grace

As we live out of a grace-shaped identity, God's undeserved love and acceptance is constantly present and working in our lives. His grace is not something that touches our lives a couple of times and then is removed; it becomes the very world in which we live every moment of our lives. Sometimes we have the mistaken idea that after we're initially forgiven of our sins because of God's grace, we're then supposed to live the rest of our lives out of our own strength. This misunderstanding completely misses the point of grace. The very grace through which God forgives us and allows us to begin the journey with Him in the first place *continues* to give us our identity and to transform our lives.

It's a dangerous turn that we take in our journey with God when we begin to believe that the things we do *make* us Christian. *God's grace* makes us Christian; what we do *gives expression* to what God has done and is doing in our lives. Just as we were dependent upon God's grace the moment we began the journey, we continue to be dependent upon God's grace every moment of the journey. The same grace that allows us to be Christian in the first place allows us to *continue* to be Christian moment by moment. Why would we begin the journey by placing our dependence upon the acceptance and forgiveness of God but then continue by placing our dependence upon our own performance? Why not *continue* in God's grace?

Continuing in God's Grace: Transformation, Strength, and Renewal

As we live in the world of God's grace, God continues to transform us. He changes us step by step into the very image of Jesus Christ. Far from a "fast-food" religion in which God gives us a bag of supplies and sends us on our way, He goes *with us* on the journey. As we journey in God's presence and live in His world of grace, neither walking ahead of Him nor walking behind Him, but walking *with* Him, God molds us, teaches us, and leads us. As He transforms us, we'll experience a wholeness and completeness in our lives that only He can provide.

For whatever reason, we don't often talk publicly about the weaknesses, inadequacies, and struggles that we often continue to experience in our lives as Christians. We're often silent and cover up. However, because God did not come to take away our humanity, but rather to *take on* our humanity, we all face weakness, experience inadequacies, and have struggles each day. Often when we encounter weaknesses, we climb into the grandstands and become "religious spectators," watching a few people we think are flawless and have no struggles as they run the race. We say to ourselves, "If only it weren't for that certain area of my life, or if only it weren't for that inadequacy in my life, I could be a super-Christian like them." Over time, we even come to think of ourselves as second-class Christians, or worse yet, "failures."

Like our ancestor Paul, over and over we pray that God will take away our weaknesses, get rid of our inadequacies, and remove our struggles. However, God's answer to these things is not the same as our answer. Our answer is for weakness to be absent from our lives; God's answer is for *Him* to be present in our lives. Our answer is for struggles to be taken away; His answer is for *Him* to join us where we are in the middle of our struggles. God says to us just what He said to Paul: "My *grace* is enough for you, because my power is made perfect in weakness" (2 Corinthians 12:9, author's paraphrase). The ultimate answer to our weaknesses, inadequacies, and struggles is not their absence, but God's presence. The same grace by which God forgives us also gives us His strength to face our weaknesses, His resources to face our inadequacies, and His victory to face our struggles.

Anyone who has journeyed for even a short while with God is also familiar with those times of dryness that come along. More than a change in our emotions, there seem to be times in our journey with God when the passing of time, busy schedules, everyday routine, and pressures of life lead to a sense of emptiness. Like a car whose fuel has been running below empty for several miles, we feel as if we're making the journey on the fumes of a past experience. God even seems to have become more remote, and our journey with God seems to have been put on "pause." Just like a follower of God who experienced this dryness many centuries ago, we cry out, "As a deer longs for flowing streams, so my soul longs for you, O God" (Psalm 42:1). In these dry times, our response can easily be to find ways to help us quickly overcome the dryness. We look for a quick emotional or intellectual jolt. However, these jolts don't stop the thirst; they just lead us to see how thirsty we really are. In the same way that only God can forgive us, only God can renew us and satisfy our thirst. In those dry times, we place our trust in the same God who transforms us and strengthens us.

Responding to Grace

So if God through His grace forgives us, gives us a new identity, transforms us, strengthens us, and renews us, where do *we* fit in? Do we just stand by and do nothing? Ultimately our part in God's alternative world of grace is found in our *response.* The question that faces us is "How do we respond to the grace of God?"

On one hand, we can respond by continuing to live life as if we forgive ourselves, transform ourselves, give ourselves a new identity, strengthen ourselves, and renew ourselves. In other words, we can continue to live life as if everything were still up to how well we perform and what we can accomplish.

On the other hand, we can respond to God's grace with trust, depending on *God* and God alone to forgive us, to transform us, to strengthen us, and to renew us. We respond to God's grace with a complete dependence upon what *He* can do. Trusting God with *all* of our lives is simply living out our *grace-shaped identity* in the first place. When we respond in dependence on God, we're simply *living out* who we already are!

Jesus talked about this response of trust in His Sermon on the Mount. (See Matthew 6:24-34.) He understood that we all build certain "systems" to provide us

life. He also understood that ultimately we'll all have one
source on which we finally depend to give us life. That
source will either be *ourselves* and all the little systems
we create, or that source will be God. He continues by
saying that those of us who live in God's *alternative*
kingdom and place our ultimate trust in God will not
spend our lives worrying about providing life for ourselves. He describes the way God provides for birds and
fields and says that if God shows that much care for
birds and grass, how much more will He take care of us.
In other words, *God will provide.* We can trust Him with
all of our life. Jesus concludes by telling us to find first
God's *alternative* kingdom—a world in which we trust
God completely to be God. As we come to see that life really does come to us as a gift from God, we will give up
trying to make all the pieces fit by how well we perform
and by what we can accomplish. We respond to God's
grace by simply receiving life, accepting life, and trusting God to give us life.

As Adam came to see grace as the heartbeat of this
alternative Kingdom, he realized that God was calling
him to trust Him completely as the *source* for his life.
Adam knew that God had forgiven him, but he also knew
that he continued to create "systems" in which he placed
his trust. He still found performance and accomplishment at the heart of much of what he was doing even for
God. Adam felt divided. He felt as though he had one foot
in God's alternative kingdom of grace and another foot in
the world of achievement. On one hand he trusted God,
but on the other hand he continued to trust what he
could do himself. Little by little, he "committed" some of
those "systems" to God.

But Adam began to sense that God was calling him to
something deeper than committing "things" now and

then. God was calling him to an undivided walk—a life of complete trust in God. Adam was being called to *be* who he already was: a graced, blessed, gifted child of God.

Reflecting on Our Journey with God

1. In everyday life, where do we see people living in a world of performance, achievement, and self-sufficiency?

2. In what ways do we tend to depend on our own performance and willpower in our journey with God?

3. Why is it sometimes tough to accept the whole concept of grace? Why might we accept the fact that we're forgiven by Christ through His grace but then live the rest of our lives as if everything were still up to us?

4. As you continue to journey with God, in what ways is He challenging you to go on by responding to His grace with trust and dependence?

5. To further explore what the Bible has to say about the grace of God and our response of trust, read Deuteronomy 8:12-18; Matthew 6:25-34; Romans 3:21-26; 2 Corinthians 12:8-10; and Ephesians 2:1-10.

*You also must consider yourselves dead
to sin and alive to God in Christ Jesus.*
—Romans 6:11

Wanted: Dead and Alive

While Adam knew that God had forgiven him
and that he was in a growing relationship with God, he
struggled more and more with the idea of an *undivided*
walk with God. Periodically he committed to God certain
things like relationships, his job, school, extracurricular
activities, and the future. However, he began to realize
that living life in the alternative Kingdom totally in the
grace of God went beyond the commitment of "things."
Adam knew that to truly live by grace was to trust God
with *all* of his life. However, he continued to find himself
creating "systems" to provide life for himself. It seemed
that when he would commit one "system" to God, he just
turned around and found another one with which to re-
place it.

Adam often asked himself, "Why do I keep on creating these 'systems' to provide life, acceptance, and security for myself? What in the world lies at the heart of all
of those systems I keep creating?" Soon he began to discover that at the very heart of each system that he had
created, whether it be relationships, money, personal ac-

complishments, acceptance and popularity, or even religious duties, was the mistaken idea that he could ultimately be self-sufficient and that he could rely on his own performance and his own achievements to give himself life. Although Adam knew that he was forgiven by God through His grace, living every moment of life *in* God's grace was another matter. Perhaps the ultimate answer to the question that Adam had been asking for months, "What happens *now?*" was found in *living* life, all of life, *in* God's grace. The ultimate response to God's grace would be a complete trust in the God who provided life, who provides life, and who will continue to provide life. The grace of God that forgave him could invade his life so deeply that Adam could truly be *dead* to his old life of accomplishments and performance and live a new life of grace and mercy!

Adam had heard people use the language of "dying to sin" and "living to God" before; however, he always found those terms odd. It just didn't make sense to him how a person could be "dead" but at the same time be "alive." As he continued to struggle with that question, he was soon to discover just what it meant to be both dead and alive.

It was the next to the last game of the season for the Riverdale Wildcats. Adam had been back from his injury for just a couple weeks. The team had dominated most of the season and had picked up only one loss. Earlier in the day, students with face paint and noisemakers had put on a massive pep rally in the gym. The Wildcats were playing their crosstown rivals, who were also looking toward a spot in the playoffs. This game was going to be huge. Not only were local news crews on the sidelines, but several college scouts were also on hand. As the team sat in the locker room, the coach went over last-minute details. An excitement mixed with nervous tension filled the room.

Although the game started out slowly, it took a dramatic turn a couple of minutes before halftime. Adam was on one defensive end; Fred Wilson was on the other. While Fred was one of the best players on the team, he hadn't started at the defensive end much. On the third down and five yards to go, the other team ran a simple option that the Wildcats had spent months learning to defend. Tackling the running back, Adam managed to knock the ball loose. It bounced out of four different hands before winding up in Fred's hands.

After picking up the ball, Fred began to run the wrong way. Astonished team members began chasing him and yelling his name. The confused defensive end ran straight ahead. Strutting into the wrong end zone, he began to dance in celebration. In front of his friends, family, and news cameras, Fred had scored his first touchdown . . . in the wrong zone!

Fred's celebration quickly became a nightmare as he realized what had happened. Time stood still. As the team surrounded Fred, they slowly walked back to the sideline. In a matter of moments, he had gone from being a hero to being nothing more than a big joke. As the team walked into the locker room, no one said a word, not even the coach. Everyone knew that Fred's football career was over before it ever started. Taking off his shoulder pads for the final time and beginning to clear out his locker, Fred's dreams of playing college football had evaporated so quickly.

As the coach began to explain the strategy for the next half, he never mentioned what had happened. As the team started to suit back up, the coach gave final instructions. Looking over at Fred, whose face was buried

in his hands, the coach said, "The same team that started the first half will be starting the second half." Everyone turned in disbelief—Fred was getting a second
chance!

With a newfound confidence, the team walked back
onto the field. Having mixed emotions, Fred knew that
all eyes were on him. More than anything else, he wanted to get back onto the field and make his coach proud.
He had been given a second chance, and he wanted to
make the most of it. His anxiety turned into focused en-
ergy, and his embarrassment was left behind in the locker room, where the coach believed in him enough to give
him a second chance.

Throughout the next 30 minutes Fred became un-
stoppable. When the clock hit zero, the Wildcats were up
14 points, and Fred Wilson would never be the same person. In the second half, he managed to sack the quarterback twice, create a fumble, and make seven tackles. In
every way imaginable, Fred took the second chance and
never looked back. Although he never lost his nickname,
Fred "Wrong Way" Wilson, he went on to have an incredible career for the Wildcats and even got a shot at his
dream of playing college football.

The next day an article on Fred's remarkable turnaround appeared in the newspaper. When asked about
the turnaround, he had responded, "I was given a second
chance when I didn't deserve or expect it. That chance
made all the difference in the world. I found my confidence in knowing that the coach believed in me enough
to send me back out there to play and to remain a part
of his team." The undeserved second chance given by the
coach had turned defeat into victory and the wrong way
into the right way.

The U-Turn of Grace

At one time or another, all of us have had experiences like Fred's performance in the first half of the game. We went in the wrong direction, lost our way, and failed miserably. At times we've found ourselves without a second chance. Therefore, we remained in the agony of defeat. In our "real world," undeserved second chances are as rare as a defensive end scoring for the other team. The opportunity to be put in the "right direction" is usually unheard of. We are much more familiar with a world of "Three strikes and you're out" or "For every mistake there is an equal punishment."

However, just when we settle into a world in which we think the game is over and our failure leads us to clean out our locker, we hear the amazing news about God's alternative world of grace, a world where unexpected and undeserved second chances are extended. In this world of grace, we have seen that the poor are rich, the weak are strong, empty people are filled, and sinners are made saints! In this world of grace, our worlds are totally turned around. In God's kingdom, not only are we taken from running in the wrong direction, but we are turned in the right direction and given the strength to continue running in that direction.

Adam was increasingly coming to see just how deep and life-changing God's grace was in his life. He began to understand the optimism of God's grace for living out a consistent and growing journey. God's grace truly freed Adam from living his life according to the rules of what other people might call the "real world" and to live his life as an authentic citizen of God's alternative kingdom.

The grace of God worked two directions in his life, much like that of a U-turn. In fact, he began to refer to his journey with God as "the U-turn of grace." On the one hand, like the coach's reaction to Fred, God had taken Adam off the wrong direction. He had put an end to the old life of depending on his own performance, his ability to "measure up," and his personal accomplishments. At the same time, God had set Adam in the right direction. He had opened up a new life of forgiveness, acceptance, and mercy. As a result of God's U-turn of grace, Adam was *dead* to sin and *alive* to God!

Wanted: Dead!

The grace of God directly affects our old life. God rescues us from our old life of sin, from a lifestyle of being the creator and provider of our own lives. Going deeper than forgiving us of our disobedient acts, God also delivers us from the endless cycle of living life as if everything were up to us. There was no way for Fred to experience victory in the second half of the game until the direction in which he was running in the first was turned around and left in the past. In order for Fred to embrace the second half, the first half had to be released; it had to "die." Refusing to live under his identity of the defeat in the first half, Fred became a new player in the second half. Ultimately, as Fred had stated, this turnaround was completely based upon the gracious act of the coach. In the same way, the grace of God allows our old direction of self-sufficiency and self-reliance to "die" and to be left behind, permitting us to find our new life and identity in a world in which God is the source of *all* of life.

We face one huge problem, however. All of us from the time we were young children have lived under the mistaken idea that ultimately life really *is* up to us. How can we ever convince ourselves of anything any different? How can we ever die to this old way of living? We often say to ourselves, "I've tried and tried, and I just can't seem to bring that old world to an end." And we're exactly right! In the same way that Fred did not simply convince himself to turn around—it took the *gracious* act of his coach—God's grace opens our eyes to the wrong direction and allows us to be nailed to a cross—to die!

More than simply accepting the events that transpired on the Cross nearly 2,000 years ago, we're invited to join Jesus on the Cross and to die as well! To join Jesus on the Cross is for us to be emptied of all of our attempts to save ourselves. To be crucified with Christ is for our minds to be freed from the false mind-set that we could ever even begin to provide life for ourselves even through our religious attempts. As we are dead to a life of putting our trust in how well we can perform, how much we can accomplish, and what we can achieve, we become alive in a world in which our total dependence and trust is in what Jesus Christ has done. What Jesus did is *enough* to provide life! We come to place our trust in nothing more and in nothing less. Realizing that there is no new life through our attempts, we die to all of those attempts—even those attempts to prove ourselves worthy to God. We can then exclaim with our ancestors, "I have been crucified with Christ; and it is no longer I who live, but it is Christ who lives in me. And the life I now live in the flesh I live by faith [trust] in the Son of God, who loved me and gave himself for me" (Galatians 2:19-20). As we are dead to our old worlds of self-sufficiency and personal achievement, we find a brand-new life in the radically *alternative* kingdom of God's grace. We are alive to God.

Commitment vs. Surrender

When we hear God's gracious invitation to *die* to our old world of performance, our response is often to com-

mit certain things to God. We believe that the more we
commit, the better a Christian we'll be. However, the call
to "die" is not simply a call to give up more of our
"stuff" to God. The call to "die" is ultimately a call to
trust God completely with *our very lives.* He wants us!
Perhaps the best word we could use for our response to
this type of call is "surrender."

The difference between surrender and commitment is
found in the focus of our attention. As we continue to focus upon our own self-sufficiency and performance, we
see God as an important "part" of our life. We even commit certain portions of our life to Him. However, the
cross remains just one of many things strapped to our
backs. We attempt to hold the cross on one shoulder
while keeping our other shoulder in our old world of self-
sufficiency and performance.

This approach, however, is ultimately impossible. We
cannot keep one foot in a world of dying to self-sufficiency and the other foot in a world of living by self-sufficiency. When we die, *we're dead!*

To surrender our lives into the hands of God is to
give up the life of dividedness, in which we trust God for
part of life and our own selves for other parts of life,
and actually trust God to be God of our lives—completely!
To *surrender* our lives into the hands of God is to give
up the game of give-and-take in which we continue to be
in control of "handing things over" to God. To surrender
is to find our very existence totally in Christ! If we were
to dare such a radical trust in God, our lives would move
from the self-centered focus of what "one more thing"
we might give up to God to a God-centered focus in which
we are completely found *in Him.* Ultimately God calls us
beyond commitment to a world of complete trust and
wholehearted surrender. As we live in this kingdom of

God, a kingdom in which God and God alone is truly King, we discover what we were meant to be in the first place—alive to God!

Wanted: Alive!

Not only did the coach bring an end to Fred's running in one direction, but he gave him the opportunity of a brand-new start and of running in a whole new direction. So much greater than Fred's "new opportunity," God's grace allows us to cross over from what was a losing first half to a transformed second half. We're given not only a "new opportunity" but also a "new life." As we die to our old world of self-reliance, we discover the indescribable joy of freedom that comes by complete trust in God as the One who provides life. As our old world of self-sufficiency is nailed to the cross of Jesus, we die only to discover a whole new life in the alternative kingdom of God.

We come to realize and to celebrate that what everyone else had been calling the "real world" was not the real world after all. In fact, the world that bases life upon self-sufficiency, performance, and achievements is nothing more than a make-believe world. It has been false all along! We now come to discover what truly is the *real* world. The Creator of this world has intended a whole other way from the beginning of time. As *alternative* as this kingdom of God may seem to others, it has been God's *real* world all along. We have not only discovered it but are *living in* it!

It is as if creation has begun all over again. We now live out our new identity as a whole new kind of humanity who continue to be dependent upon God's breathing into us. We live out this incredible identity of being the graced, forgiven, and blessed children of God by no longer trying to earn life as a prize or reward. We now simply receive life moment by moment as a gift from our Creator and Provider. And in the same way that God has loved us, we now love others.

Often we seem to think that the sole purpose of God's grace is to forgive us initially from sin. It is almost as if we view God's grace as a holy shower that washed us clean sometime in the past. From then on, God's grace is just something of the past. In this mind-set, God forgave us, but from now on we depend upon our own strength, power, and performance to maintain our relationship with Him. However, in this new life that we have with God, God's grace is much more powerful than simply doing something one time in the past. God's grace not only forgives us from sin but also makes us *alive to God.* God's grace is not a one-time shower that we took in the past; it is the very air we breathe as we live out our lives. God's grace not only took us from running in the wrong direction in the past but also sets us and continues to move us in a new direction. God's grace *continues* to breathe life into our existence so that nothing in our lives goes unaffected.

It's impossible to receive the grace of God into our lives and remain as we once were. We just can't keep running the same old direction! He will continue to transform us, to teach us, and to lead us into new adventures. By God's grace we began the journey, and by God's grace we continue to make the journey. We live in God's grace; we journey in God's grace; and we keep our lives open to God's incredibly life-changing grace!

God invites us to let go and to trust Him *with all of our lives.* We've trusted Him to forgive us of our sins; we've trusted Him with various areas of our lives. We can also trust Him *completely* with the *entirety* of our lives. He wants us to know the fullness of new life that He has to give as we trust God and God alone to be God! As we hear His trustworthy call and as we're assured of His strength and power in our lives, will we trust Him?

⚠ Reflecting on Our Journey with God

1. Where in everyday life do we see people performing one role for a part of their day or week and then another role for the rest of their day or week?

2. Why do we often find ourselves with one foot in the everyday world of performance and trying harder and another foot in God's alternative kingdom of grace?

3. What is the relationship between surrendering our lives to God and trusting Him as the source of our lives?

4. In your journey with God, how might He be calling you now to go on and to die to a world of self-sufficiency in order to live in a world of complete dependence on Him?

5. To further explore what the Bible has to say about being dead and alive, read Romans 6:1-14; 2 Corinthians 5:15-17; Galatians 2:19-21; Ephesians 2:1-10; Colossians 2:12-15; 3:1-11.

Part 3

Celebrating Our Identity

> *Beloved, I do not consider that I have made it my own; but this one thing I do: forgetting what lies behind and straining forward to what lies ahead, I press on toward the goal for the prize of the heavenly call of God in Christ Jesus.*
>
> —Philippians 3:13-14

Going On: Living the Journey

Adam had always been intrigued by stories of famous explorers. He would imagine persons like Christopher Columbus sitting on the beach at night, looking over the ocean and imagining what was over the horizon. Often consumed with the hope of a world beyond anything they had ever experienced, some of these explorers, Adam imagined, were ridiculed for looking beyond what seemed to be the impossible. Their vision seemed to pose a threat to the familiar, comfortable world of people without a vision.

Adam would imagine these explorers as they would pack up, say their good-byes, take a deep breath, and step onto the boat without ever looking back. Trusting in the skill of the ship's builders, these people dared to venture outside of the safe harbor. The days at sea were spent navigating, finding best routes, reading maps, and adjusting the sails according to the shifting winds, winds that could be both a worst enemy that could throw the ship off course and a best friend that could move the ship farther ahead.

Adam would imagine how slowly time would pass on the ship. Some days would be eventful; most days would be no different from the day before. During the early days at sea, many crewmembers would wake up early and run to the deck to see if land were in sight. After several weeks, however, many would begin to grow impatient. They would even begin to entertain the question "What if we're just fooling ourselves? What if there is no land? What if we spend the rest of our lives on the ocean?" As time would go on, life on the ship would repeat the endless cycle of remembering things that were taken for granted back home, maintaining the ship's course seemingly to nowhere, and returning to sleep. Although land was nowhere in sight, the captain would never put down the scope; nothing deterred his focus. He seemed to know that a new world lay just beyond the horizon.

Adam imagined that ordinary morning when the young man keeping watch suddenly spotted what he thought to be land. In a matter of moments, incredible celebration broke out on the ship as the unknown sailors became famous explorers. Everything for which they had dreamed, prayed, and worked was looking right at them. Having struggled against overwhelming odds, these explorers were staring a new world in the face. The world that others never imagined existed had been found!

On the shore, with tears in his eyes, the captain of the crew would thrust the flag into the ground, fall to his knees, and stake his claim in a new homeland. At that moment he had to make one of the most important decisions in the world: Would he settle down or move ahead? If he were simply to stop at where he was, the explorer

would make one of the greatest mistakes that could ever
be made. Becoming comfortable and settled, he would fail
to realize that the discovery had just *begun*. Only a tiny
piece of a new world was known. This new world on
which the explorer had stepped foot now beckoned him
to move ahead!

Called to a Lifelong Journey

The more Adam came to understand the relationship
that he shared with God, the more he realized just how
similar that relationship was to the life of the explorer.
When he had first accepted God's grace and forgiveness
in his life, Adam thought that he had "arrived" and that
all discoveries had been made. However, he was beginning to see that really he had *just begun* life in God's
world of grace. A whole new world was waiting to be ex-
plored, experienced, and celebrated. If he were ever to
fully discover what a dynamic relationship with God was
all about, Adam was going to have to leave the safety of
the shore, refuse to get comfortable with his initial discovery, and venture into the future with God. Having become a citizen of God's alternative kingdom, he would
now spend a lifetime exploring, growing, and making
new discoveries in this incredible world of God's grace.

Like Adam, we are called to the same lifelong journey with God. Once we've discovered and accepted God's
grace in our lives, we're invited to venture beyond the
familiar and secure shore and to walk into the future
with God. Hanging around the shore of our initial experience with God, perhaps wanting Him to give us a repeat
performance of that initial experience from time to time,
we fail to see that God calls us to move forward. Thinking that we've arrived at a final destination so that we
can sit back and go no farther misses the point that our

walk with God is not a static religion but a dynamic relationship. As we dare to venture ahead in God's alternative new world, we will learn truths we never dreamed of, we will grow in ways we never thought, and we will make discoveries that we never imagined!

As we live in God's story, the most common punctuation mark is not a period, a question mark, or even an exclamation point. Sure—there are times when we come to the end of a stretch in the journey, times like graduation or heading off to college. At these times it seems that a period is placed at the end of our story. There are other times that we face questions and uncertainties about our future. During these times, question marks seem to abound. Then there are those incredible moments of celebration when God has opened doors and supplied needs, and exclamation points are plentiful. However in God's story, beyond every period, beyond every question mark, and beyond every exclamation point is an *ellipsis,* a "dot, dot, dot." Nowhere in our journey with God is the story over; there is always another line to be written and another chapter to be added. In God's story, an ellipsis is found everywhere we turn. The relationship we share with God is an open-ended journey. When we come to a dead end, God opens doors to a new tomorrow. When our mind is clouded with questions and all we see is uncertainty, God makes a way through the impossible. When the celebration of victory is over, God provides new challenges for the future.

What took place in the prayer you made at an altar, or in the experience you had at a summer camp, or in the encounter you had with God at a retreat goes much deeper than simply getting a ticket stamped to get you into heaven and is much more dynamic than settling down at a destination. You started the lifetime adventure

of "being on the road" with God. In this journey there is
no such thing as simply "standing still." You are always
moving on into the future with God. In fact, the great
way we celebrate our identity as people on a journey
with God is by *going on.*

Presence over Road Maps

Since we're in a lifelong journey with God, God's direction for our lives is not found by getting His "road
map" that gives us all the details of where to go. We often act as if God is playing a game with us in which He
stands on a chair with a road map in His hand and tells
us to jump a little higher, pray a little harder, and seek a
little more. If we finally try hard enough, then we'll get
His road map for our future. But God never plays that
kind of mind game with us! God is not into dangling a
map of His will over our heads until we jump high
enough or try hard enough to get it. If God were to give
us a road map, we would trust the map rather than God.

Instead, God gives us the most incredible thing we
could have on this journey—He gives us His presence! In
the journey we make with God, we *never* walk alone. God
goes with us. Moment by moment, step by step, as we
walk with God, He guides us, instructs us, and opens the
door to the next chapter of life. Rather than experiencing
God's direction in our lives as a road map, we come to
know God's direction as we live each moment of our day
in His presence. One thing we can count on in this journey: God will be faithful. Therefore, we can trust Him!

Facing Frustration, Weakness, and Sin

God desires that we walk with Him in total honesty.
This means that we don't cover up. There's no reason to
put a mask on as we walk with God. Christianity has

nothing to do with learning how to "fake it." When we face frustrations, when we have fears, and when we experience pains or hurts in life, we can be totally *honest* and completely real in front of God. God never intended to give us a religion of masks and costumes. He does not want us to play the game of cover-up. Rather, He intends for us to be open and honest in our relationship with Him. God is not scared to hear our fears, our frustrations, and our hurts. Rather, we can see them, admit them, and be honest to God about them. When we don't understand God, when we have questions about why certain things are happening, and even when we feel that God is far off from what we're experiencing, God can handle hearing the way we feel.

In our weaknesses and struggles, we are also called to live a life of honesty. Rather than pretending that we have no weaknesses or finding ways to hide them, we can look at them honestly and admit them. Just as putting a bandage on an injury will not heal the injury, hiding our wounds, our weaknesses, and our struggles does not bring healing. Jesus did not come first to *take away* our weaknesses and wounds; rather, He came to *enter into* life with us and to *share* the real life of our weaknesses and wounds. In this lifelong journey with God, we come to discover that God's grace and love are enough in our weaknesses. Rather than covering up, God calls us to honesty!

We're also invited to be honest with sin. We're called to live a life free from sinning. However, if we do sin, the answer is not to cover up or pretend that everything is still fine. In our journey with God, we can turn to God and admit, or confess, our sin. Confession may be one of the toughest things for some of us to do. However, if we simply call sin a "mistake," if we learn to live with sin by covering it up, or if we come to ignore the seriousness of sin altogether, we will not experience the incredibly honest and open relationship with God that He wants us to have with Him. We will find ourselves hiding from God and from each other. But when we live a life of honesty and confession, we share in a beautiful and open relationship with God and with each other.

Making the Journey—Together!

As we journey with God, we soon come to make one of the most amazing discoveries: there are many other persons on the journey with us! Not only are there some well-known characters with whom we share God's story, but there are also millions of not-so-famous people who have lived before us, as well as people of different languages, cultures, and nationalities scattered all over the world today. The journey we make with God is definitely not a journey of just "Jesus and me." In fact, God never intended for us to make this journey alone. Even when we feel most alone, we're a part of a huge family who have lived before us, who are living all over the world today, and who will live after us. We're a part of an incredible family who have an amazing family history; this family is called the Church.

The way that Jesus has been roaming the earth for 2,000 years is not through isolated individuals but through a community of people who journey together. *Together* we're the Body of Jesus Christ—not alone. Each of us is a different part of that Body, and each of us has a different function. Some of us are eyes; some of us are noses; some of us are fingers; and some of us are ears. But only *together* are we the complete Body of Jesus. The way we see Jesus and the way the world sees Jesus is through *us—together!* We never make this journey by ourselves. We join the hands and the lives and the hearts and the voices of millions of people throughout history and throughout the world who travel with God. We make this journey *together!*

Our Response on the Journey: Trust!

As we accept God's grace and enter into a lifelong journey with God, the exploration and the discoveries have just begun. Rather than putting our stake down and settling at the shore, we journey moment by moment in God's presence into His future. Making the journey in honesty and openness and traveling *together* with an amazingly diverse family, we experience the most incredible lifetime adventure possible.

If there's any one word that best describes *how* we live out the journey, it would be one we've already encountered several times, one that describes *how* we responded to God's grace in the first place. That word is "trust." Trust in God goes deeper than convincing ourselves not to worry but to "be happy." Trust is realizing and accepting that the source of all of life is outside of us and in Jesus Christ. However, trust is not only accepting but *living* according to the reality that the source of everything good in our lives is God. We live our lives as a celebration that we cannot give life to ourselves; only God can give us that. Trust is celebrating the fact that you and I were never created to be gods, nor are we gods now, nor will we *ever* be gods. Trust is depending on the one who gave us life in the first place to continue to give us life, day by day, hour by hour, moment by moment. Ultimately, trust is our response to God's grace. The way we make this journey with God is simply by *trusting* God—to be God!

Many of the hurdles we face in our journey with God are found in our attempt to take matters into our own hands rather than to trust God. Often we tend to focus on what *we* did at a camp or how *we* prayed at an altar and expect for our performance to transform us and bring us the immediate results we desire. Or we tend to focus on the religion of significant people in our lives, simply plugging their religion into our lives and trying to make that religion work for us. As a result, we expect our performance to give us a growing walk with God. Or we tend to focus on making Jesus a model whom we can try harder and harder in our own strength to be like. We think that finally someday we'll be able to perform well enough that we'll be like Jesus. Once again, the result is a life in which *our* performance takes center stage. Or we tend to plug Jesus into *our* world, finding a significant place to fit Him into our lives and on our priority lists. But again we find ourselves right back at our own performance, with Jesus "attached" to our lives.

Rather than continuing to depend upon our own attempts and determination to "try harder the next time," what if we were simply to depend upon the God who invited us to participate in His alternative kingdom in the first place to *continue* to change us, to lead us, and to instruct us? This complete dependency is the lifestyle of trust that is lived out by simply walking with God, moment by moment, step by step. The way we celebrate our identity as the graced children of God is first in a lifelong journey of *trust*. As we journey with God moment by moment, step by step, we keep our lives in a posture of openness to God's grace. Throughout our journey with God, we remain in a position of dependency in which God's life-changing grace can continue to transform us, lead us, and instruct us. There are various practices that Christians have carried out for centuries that can prepare us to be in such an "open position" to God's life-changing grace. In the final chapter we will briefly explore these practices.

Reflecting on Our Journey with God

1. Where in day-to-day life do we see people arrive at some point in their lives and then decide to stop where they are? What might be some reasons that a person would stop where he or she is and not go any further?

2. Why do we sometimes get to a point in our relationship with God that we just stop? What happens in our walk with God when we do this?

3. Why is a life of honesty so important in a dynamic and growing relationship with God? Do you find it toughest to be honest with God about (a) the way you're feeling, (b) the struggles you're facing, or (c) sin you've committed?

4. What roles does community play in our walk with God?

5. As you continue to make the journey with God, in what ways might He be challenging you to go on by giving up the search for a preplanned road map for your life, and instead, living each moment in His presence?

6. To further explore what the Bible has to say about our going on in an honest and growing walk with God, read Genesis 17:1; Psalms 42; 43; 139:23-24; Philippians 3:12-16; 1 John 1:5—2:2; and Hebrews 12:1-4.

Finally, beloved, whatever is true, whatever is honorable, whatever is just, whatever is pure, whatever is pleasing, whatever is commendable, if there is any excellence and if there is anything worthy of praise, think about these things.

—Philippians 4:8

All of us . . . are being transformed into the same image from one degree of glory to another; for this comes from the Lord, the Spirit.

—2 Corinthians 3:18

Remembering and Becoming

As we set out on the journey with God and with other participants in God's story, we're faced with the question "So how do we live our lives? What are we supposed to *do?*" Often our first response to this question is for us to set up a list of dos, don'ts, and how-tos. However, when we reduce our relationship with God to a simple list of things to do, the journey can easily lose its dynamic and growing nature. When our primary focus is on our "list of dos, don'ts, and how-tos," we can easily end up turning a relationship based upon God's grace into a relationship based on our performance. The journey can become static and routine until we're doing nothing more than "going through the motions."

With our radically new identity in the story of God, we very definitely have ways of living and behaving. However, the very heart of our identity tells us that in our journey with God, everything we *do* comes first from what God *has already done* in our lives. All our actions and behaviors come from *who we are,* our identity, in Jesus! Therefore, if we're ever to know what we should do, we first must know what God has done in us. Coming to know what God has done in our lives has been the primary focus of the journey we've made over the past few pages.

As we know what God has done, we come to know *who* we are and *who* we're becoming! At the heart of living out the journey with God and with each other is *remembering* and *becoming.* Perhaps this is the best way to sum up what we are called to do on this journey. Who are we? As we've discovered, we are *participants* in the alternative Kingdom of grace in which we're called to have an undivided trust not in ourselves but in God. Who are we becoming? Step by step and by God's grace, we're being changed into the very likeness of Jesus Christ himself!

Remembering

Every step along the journey, we're called to remember who we are. Ultimately, we're people of grace, which means that our identity is not based first on our performance but on what God has done. We live our lives realizing that our "doing" does not *give* us a walk with God, but rather it's the *expression* of our walk with God. Our lifestyle is the overflow of *who* we are! The Christian lifestyle is not a drudgery of doing things in order to become Christian. The Christian lifestyle is the celebration of our identity. Because we're people in a gracious and trusting relationship with God, we live our lives in gracious and trusting ways. Because together we're the

Body of Jesus Christ, we live our lives together in ways that reflect Jesus Christ. As people on a journey with God, there are very definite ways that we live. However, we live those very definite ways because of *who we are* and because of *who God is creating us to be!*

In the busyness of our everyday lives as the "real world" squeezes in upon us, we can easily forget who we are. Even though we know deep down that we're citizens of God's *alternative kingdom,* we can once again quickly buy into the slogan "If it's going to be, it's up to me." Faced with making the team, making the grade, making friends, and making a name, we find ourselves again living as if a successful life really were dependent upon our performance. In the midst of a world of achievement, *remember* who you are! In the midst of a world of performance, don't forget your identity! Who you are is first dependent upon God and what God has done. You are a person of God's grace, love, and forgiveness. You are a participant in an alternative Kingdom. You are a member of a community that sees all of life differently. Never forget who you are! Refuse to compromise your identity! Be willing to admit that you belong to the *alternative* kingdom of God. Dare to turn away from a world of personal achievements and accomplishments. Continue to be a person with a "grace-shaped identity." Be who you are as a graced and forgiven child of God.

Throughout our family history, there have been many ways that our ancestors have been reminded of who they were. Like our ancestors, we allow ourselves to be placed in situations that help us remember who we are. We desire to be in circumstances and places, we desire to hear sounds and see sights, and we desire to be with other people that can more readily remind us of who we are. We allow our minds that are being transformed to focus on those things that are true, honorable, just, pure, pleasing, commendable, excellent, and praise-worthy (Philippians 4:8).

When we come together with others to worship God, we're particularly reminded of our identity. The focus of worship is God. In worship we see God for who He really is. We see that He's a God of love, grace, and forgive-ness. When we come together with other Christians to worship God, we're reminded that we're loved, graced, and forgiven. Through songs, prayers, scripture reading, preaching, and the taking of Communion, we're remind-ed over and over again of who God is, what He's done, what He's doing, and what He'll do. In each part of a worship service we participate in what God is doing. As we participate, we're reminded of and we come to under-stand more clearly our roles as characters in the story of God. In worship we come face-to-face with God, and we're reminded of who we are in light of God.

As we study the Bible, we're also reminded of our identity. Reading God's Word is often like listening to fami-ly stories from grandparents and great-grandparents. As we hear such stories over and over, we connect to a long family line. In an even greater way, when we read the Bible, we hear our family story. We're connected to those ancestors who have participated in the story of God before us. Some of the stories of the Bible serve as memorials of great past events. These stories show us where we came from, what shaped us, and what brought us to this point. Other stories of great heroes and heroines provide us with models of how we, too, can live out our relationship with God and with each other. We look at their lives, and they set a pattern for us. Just as in the stories of our own fam-ilies, not every story in the Bible is a *memorial* of a great event or a *model* of how to act. Sometimes the stories of our ancestors are more like *mirrors*. As we hear their stories, we see ourselves more clearly. As we see the frailties, weaknesses, and shortcomings of our ancestors, we often see the same things in us. In hearing these stories, we realize that we're not the first people to face certain struggles. We're certainly not alone.

In addition to stories, there are also songs, laws, letters, and sermons in the Bible. As we read these different types of materials, we continue to look through our family scrapbook. In the songs we hear how our ancestors responded to God. In the laws we see specific ways in which our ancestors lived out their identity as God's people. In the letters we see how certain problems and questions faced by our ancestors were answered. And in the sermons, we hear relevant messages that were preached to our ancestors. In studying these materials we come face-to-face with our identity: who we are, where we came from, and how we are to be.

As we spend time with other people who are making the journey with God, we remind each other of who we are. While we very often "have fun" when we get together, we know that "getting together" has an even greater purpose behind it. When we get together with other people on the journey, we remind each other that none of us are alone. When we seem to be forgetting who we are and seem to be allowing the everyday "real world" to squeeze us back into its mold, these other people who are making the journey alongside of us remind us of our identity. Some of these persons have been on the journey much longer than we have, others are peers on the journey, and still others have just begun the journey. However, we're there for each other; we're there to remind each other of *who we are;* we're there to say, "You're not alone on this road! I'm with you!"

Becoming

In our journey with God, we not only remember who we are but also realize that God by His grace is continuing to transform us and change us into the likeness of Jesus Christ. Based on what He has done and is doing in our lives, we're also *becoming.* God has changed us, but He continues doing so. In this lifelong journey, we're continually being transformed into the likeness of Jesus Christ. However, as people of grace, we don't change ourselves. We don't put the pieces together and *make ourselves* into the likeness of Jesus. God is the one who transforms our minds and our lives. The same life-changing grace of God with which He forgave us in the first place *keeps on* working in our lives and *keeps on* changing us into the image of Jesus Christ.

However, while *God* is the one who transforms us, we don't simply stand back and do nothing. In our "becoming," we live day by day, moment by moment, in the presence of God. Various practices have served our ancestors and serve us as channels or means of God's life-changing grace. These practices themselves do not actually change us, but they put us in positions of openness in which God's grace can bring about change. Much like tilling soil, the tilling does not cause things to grow, but it does create an environment in which the seed can have a greater opportunity to grow and produce fruit. Similarly, these practices do not create a relationship with the Lord. None of these practices will *make us* Christian. They're not ends in themselves. However, they keep our lives open to the activity of God's grace in our lives. They're means to place us in a position of openness in which the grace of God can actively work.

All of these practices are expressions of a dependent and trusting relationship with God. They are also expressions of our *participation* in what Jesus Christ is doing. As we move beyond the shores of our initial encounter with God's grace, indescribable discoveries await us as we explore and participate in these practices.

The practice of prayer is the expression of our trusting and dependent walk with God. We pray out of the ongoing journey that we're in rather than simply when we're "in a pinch" or when we face a crisis. In prayer we don't simply come with a "wish list" to God and ask Him for the things we need and want, but we come to God recognizing that He alone is the source of all life. Therefore, in prayer we worship God as the source of life. We thank Him for what He's provided and the blessings He's given us. Knowing that we're no longer playing the game of self-sufficiency, we present to God the various needs of our lives and of other people's lives. Ultimately, the practice of prayer is laying our lives before God in absolute openness and dependency.

In our walk with God, we grow and mature in the practice of prayer. The disciples who lived with Jesus and watched the way He prayed asked Him to teach them how to pray. Therefore, prayer is learned. At first it may seem to be a somewhat frustrating and even awkward practice. We'll always be explorers journeying deeper and deeper into the heart of God's kingdom. Often our growth in prayer resembles communication with other people whom we're getting to know. At first we may simply discuss surface things. When we run out of things to say, we may quickly say "Amen" and go on our way. However, as we continue to grow in the practice of prayer, we move out of a surface relationship with the Lord and into a deeper communication with God. Prayer will become as much a time of waiting in God's presence as it is a time of talking to God. The practice of prayer lies at the heart of keeping our lives open to the life-changing grace of God. In so doing, we participate in communion with God.

The practice of Scripture reading reminds us that we are people with an identity. We have roots that go deep into the past. We're connected to the grand story of God. As we read scripture, the words of the pages speak into our lives, showing us that the God who has loved, forgiven, and acted in the past continues to love, forgive, and act. We're reminded that our individual stories and agendas have been swallowed up into something larger and that we ourselves are active characters in that larger drama. We come to see the situations we're in, the questions we ask, and the circumstances we face in light of God's story. As we see ourselves in light of the story of God, God opens our minds to new truths of who He is and who we are. He takes our "real worlds" in which we've settled for the way things are and shows us His *alternative* world. In the practice of Scripture reading, we participate in the grand story of God.

In the practice of worship we see God for who He really is. In worship we look beyond ourselves and our own private, individual worlds and see the *alternative* Kingdom, where God truly is God. In the hymns and choruses that we sing, in the prayers that we pray, in the scripture that we read, in the sermon that we hear, and in the Lord's Supper that we eat, the presence of God encounters us. We *see* God as He is! And as we see Him, we participate in what He's doing. Worship is not an activity of feeling better or getting an emotional boost for the week. Worship is an encounter with God. Feelings come and go, but a vision of God stays forever!

Neither is worship simply going to a performance to be entertained. It becomes easy for us in worship to imagine that the preacher and the singers are the performers, God is the "prompter," and we're the audience. But in true worship, *we* are the "performers," the preacher and the singers are the "prompters," and *God* is the "audience"! Worship is our expression of praise and adoration to God. Worship is our acknowledgement to God of who He is as our Creator and our Provider. Worship is our joining hands with the rest of God's creation to put into words and action our utter trust and dependence on God. In the practice of worship, we participate in the great drama of God!

In the practice of Christian service, we participate in the ministry of Jesus Christ. In carrying out acts of mercy, we discover that the ministry to which we are called is not "our ministry" or "our" service, but the ministry of Jesus. Jesus, not us, is the one who *continues* to change the world. While we're His instruments, the ministry of changing lives and minds and societies is *His* ministry. Christian service is not simply making the world a better place, nor is it merely doing an occasional act of kindness to other people. What makes Christian ministry *Christian* is that we're participating in what God is doing. As we carry out various acts of mercy, we discover the rich meaning of being a member of the Body of Jesus Christ. Joining hearts and hands with other people who are making the journey as well, *together* we come to understand what it means for Jesus to be roaming the earth not through a lot of individuals but through His *one Body!*

As we participate in Christlike service and acts of mercy, these become for us a means that God uses graciously to continue to transform our minds into the mind of Christ. As we *participate* in what Christ is doing, our minds are transformed. Many of us have seen the way in which God uses a mission trip or involvement in a ministry to transform the way we think. We often say it this way: "I think *my* life was changed more on that trip than the lives of the people I ministered to." What we're really saying is that God uses acts of mercy and Christian service as a means of His grace to transform our lives. In Christian service we participate in the world-changing activity of God.

A final practice that serves as a significant means of God's life-changing grace is the practice of accountability that we share with another believer or a small group of believers. In the practice of accountability, we gather together to testify to what God is doing in our lives, to share the struggles of our lives, to support each other along the path by rejoicing in the victories and encouraging in the midst of defeat, and to pray together.

As we share in accountability with other persons, we truly come to participate in the mystery of being a part of the Body of Christ. In accountability, we not only accept but celebrate in the fact that we need each other on this journey—in fact, we accept and celebrate that there is no other way to make this journey but *together* with other people.

While we often enjoy being in the presence of others, our primary purpose in the practice of accountability is not simply the "good feelings" that we have of being with our friends. In relationships of accountability, where trust is an absolute necessity, strong bonds will develop. In the midst of the deep commitments to each other in relationships of accountability, Christ must remain central in our shared accountability. Otherwise, our moments together will simply become friendly conversation or even a substitute for our shared walk with Christ rather than Christian accountability. In the practice of accountability, we participate in the truly shared life of Christian community.

In all these practices we simply continue to journey in the life-changing presence of God. Again, while these activities do not transform us, they are means of God's grace that permit our lives to be open to the transforming grace of God. In them we participate *in Jesus Christ* as we participate in communion with God, as we participate in the grand story of God, as we participate in the great drama of God, as we participate in the world-changing activity of God, and as we participate in the shared life of the community of God. Through these practices, God's grace shapes us and transforms us into the likeness of Jesus as we continue to *become* all God intends us to be!

⚠ Reflecting on Our Journey with God

1. Where in everyday life do we see the identity of a person shaping what that person does and how he or she acts?

2. Why is the following statement so important in understanding how we live out our relationship with God? *Our actions and behaviors come from who we are— our identity—in Jesus Christ.*

3. What particular activities and people are good at re-
minding you of who you are?

4. Why is it important to see the practices of prayer,
Scripture reading, worship, service, and accountability as channels or means of God's life-changing grace
in our lives?

5. In the journey you're making with God, how might He
be challenging you to go on by growing in the practices of prayer, Scripture reading, worship, service,
and accountability?

6. To further explore what the Bible says about remembering who we are and living out our identity, read
Deuteronomy 6:10-14, 20-23; Matthew 5:3-16; 6:1-
18; Romans 12:1-2; 2 Corinthians 3:17-18; Philippians 4:4-9; Ephesians 3:14-21; Colossians 3:12-17;
4:2-6; 2 Timothy 2:1-9; and Hebrews 10:19-25.

Epilogue

As Adam came to celebrate his "first birthday" in his journey with God, he realized that in answer to the question "What happens now?" his attention had been taken off himself and onto God. He came to realize that both his identity and his lifestyle were based upon God! Adam was a person of grace. Adam lived his life as a person of grace.

He also came to realize that he was on a journey—a lifelong journey! The adventure to which God had called him to participate was so much more than simply getting out onto the slopes and "going for it." It was about getting to know, spending time with, learning from, and living in the presence of his Instructor. He came not only to accept the fact but to celebrate the fact that in this journey with God *we never make it alone!* We "ride the slopes" in His presence.

Late one afternoon Adam sat down for a few minutes just to reflect on what he had learned about his identity in Christ and where he was to go from there. His reflections went something like this:

He has called you to a journey, not a destination.
Now get on the road and go.

He has called you to a change in mind and the way you think, not just a change in life and the way you act.
Now lay your mind before Him.

He has called you to a relationship, not simply a religion.
Now say, "Here I am; what do You want?"

He has called you into His world, not simply
asked you to let Him come into your world.
Now "enter in."

He has called you to be a participant, not a spectator.
Now get out of the balcony and onto the stage!

He has called you into His alternative kingdom.
Now be a citizen!

He has called you to a life of grace, not simply
to a life of trying harder in your own strength.
Now trust Him.

He has called you to die in order to live,
not simply to live and finally die.
Now take up your cross.

He has given you a whole new identity.
Now remember who you are.

He is changing you into the likeness of Jesus Christ.
Now become who He calls you to be!